Take Control with Astrology

For Julie and Carole

Teach Yourself ®

Take Control with Astrology

Lisa Tenzin-Dolma

For UK order enquiries: please contact Bookpoint Ltd,
130 Milton Park, Abingdon, Oxon OX14 4SB.
Telephone: +44 (0) 1235 827720. Fax: +44 (0) 1235 400454.
Lines are open 09.00–17.00, Monday to Saturday, with a 24-hour
message answering service. Details about our titles and how to
order are available at www.teachyourself.com

For USA order enquiries: please contact McGraw-Hill Customer
Services, PO Box 545, Blacklick, OH 43004-0545, USA.
Telephone: 1-800-722-4726. Fax: 1-614-755-5645.

For Canada order enquiries: please contact McGraw-Hill Ryerson
Ltd, 300 Water St, Whitby, Ontario L1N 9B6, Canada.
Telephone: 905 430 5000. Fax: 905 430 5020.

Long renowned as the authoritative source for self-guided learning –
with more than 50 million copies sold worldwide – the **Teach Yourself**
series includes over 500 titles in the fields of languages, crafts,
hobbies, business, computing and education.

British Library Cataloguing in Publication Data: a catalogue record
for this title is available from the British Library.

Library of Congress Catalog Card Number: on file.

First published in UK 1999 by Hodder Education, part of Hachette
UK, 338 Euston Road, London NW1 3BH.

First published in US 1999 by The McGraw-Hill Companies, Inc.

This edition published 2010.

Previously published as *Teach Yourself Astrology*

The **Teach Yourself** name is a registered trade mark of
Hodder Headline.

Copyright © 2007, 2010 Lisa Tenzin-Dolma

Typeset by Macmillan Publishing Solutions.

Printed in Great Britain for Hodder Education, an Hachette UK
Company, 338 Euston Road, London NW1 3BH, by CPI Cox &
Wyman, Reading, Berkshire RG1 8EX.

The publisher has used its best endeavours to ensure that the URLs
for external websites referred to in this book are correct and active
at the time of going to press. However, the publisher and the
author have no responsibility for the websites and can make no
guarantee that a site will remain live or that the content will remain
relevant, decent or appropriate.

Hachette UK's policy is to use papers that are natural, renewable
and recyclable products and made from wood grown in sustainable
forests. The logging and manufacturing processes are expected to
conform to the environmental regulations of the country of origin.

Impression number   10 9 8 7 6 5 4 3 2 1
Year   2014 2013 2012 2011 2010

Acknowledgements

A book which aims to simplify and make accessible the vast
subject of astrology, necessarily involves many people whom I
have learned from in the course of 28 years of study and practical
application. Although space does not permit all of these to be
named, special thanks must be extended to Brian and Penny, who
first stimulated my fascination with astrology, and to Bruno and
Louise Huber, who, many years ago, taught me the principles of
psychological astrology.

My family have been immensely supportive throughout the writing
of this book. Loving thanks and rounds of applause for their
patience go to my sister Julie; my children, Ryan, Oliver, Daniel,
Liam and Amber; my parents, Betty and Harold; and my
step-parents, Gerald and Frankie. My mother passed away
while this book was still in progress but was, throughout my life,
a huge source of love and encouragement.

Jen Govey, who generously agreed that her birth chart could be
used as an example throughout the book, read and commented
on each chapter and continually buoyed me up with her enthusiasm
and feedback. Thank you, Jen! If you want to find out more about
lovely Jen and her work, you can visit her at: www.jengovey.co.uk
or www.myspace.com/filmtopia.

Many friends have inspired and encouraged me. In particular,
Carole Negre, Rachael Eldritch-Boersen, Margret Heiligenstadt,
Shani and Bruce Hubble, Lynne Benton, Catherine Norwood-Aird
and Ivy Morgan. Thanks – you've been wonderful!

Many thanks are due to Victoria Roddam, publisher at Hodder
Education, for her patience and encouragement during the writing
process. Also to Vicky Butt and Helen Hart for their enthusiasm
while preparing the completed manuscript for publication.

Contents

Meet the author

Welcome to *Take Control with Astrology*!

I first became interested in astrology over 30 years ago, when a friend who knew of my studies of the I Ching and numerology taught me how to calculate natal charts. Astrology quickly became a passion, and this was intensified when my oldest son became seriously ill with meningitis as a baby. Despite the grave prognosis at that time, his chart indicated both the likelihood of the illness and that he would fully recover, and this proved to be true. From then on I was hooked, and went on to build up a vast collection of natal charts for people of all ages. It works well for animals, too, and, as you will discover in this book, can be a valuable key to the personality.

Technology has made astrology far more widely accessible now. Thirty years ago, charts had to be laboriously calculated mathematically and a simple miscalculation would culminate in an inaccurate natal chart. Nowadays we can create a birth chart in seconds, thanks to computers and the expertise of those who understand the intricacies of programming.

The area of astrology that has always fascinated me most is its use as a method of understanding our unique personalities and character traits in order to experience a more profound sense of self-integration, and that is the focus of *Take Control with Astrology*. Our modes of self-expression, our subtle interactions with the sometimes mysterious motivations of our inner promptings, our actions in and reactions to situations in the outside world, and our relationships with those around us are all revealed in detail in the natal chart. We can explore our strengths, understand and work to overcome our weaknesses and, ultimately, emerge from our studies with a deeper self-knowledge and the tools to more fully express the abundant resources that rest within each of us.

A question I am often asked is whether astrology implies that our lives are mapped out for us, leaving us without the choices of free will. My personal opinion is that there is no conflict between astrology and free will. Our natal charts reveal the many facets of our natures and indicate how we are most likely to respond to particular situations. Yet we are not limited by our birth charts. The capacities of the human brain are far greater than we tend to realize and make use of, and we are capable of transcending challenges which are reflected in both our natal charts and our life experiences. Through understanding our birth charts we find keys which unlock hidden doors to the self, and this allows us to blossom into the realization of far more of our innate potential.

I hope you find this book useful. After all, what could be more interesting than gaining insights into yourself that can benefit not only you but also everyone you meet!

Only got a minute?

Astrology is the oldest of the sciences, and the cycles of the moon were recorded as far back as 32,000 years ago. Yet it is also an art, because the interpretation of your birth chart involves the ability to see patterns that form a whole. Showing you how to achieve this is the aim of *Take Control with Astrology*.

Your birth chart is a map of the heavens as they appeared exactly above you at the moment and place of your birth. No two charts are the same, not even those of twins; your unique personality and the qualities which define who you are can be clearly seen by an astrologer. This use of astrology, as a key to an in-depth profile of your personality, can be immensely useful – you can discover your inner motivations and feelings, your aims and goals, your challenges and your gifts. Your birth chart shows your innate potential and how it can be fostered and developed. Studying your birth chart can help you to tap into an increasing sense of wholeness and fulfilment.

Your birth chart has the 12 astrological signs – the constellations – around the outer rim of the circle. Within the circle your chart is divided into 12 segments, called the houses. The first of these segments, the Ascendant and first house, marks your exact moment of birth. The houses represent the various areas of your life. The planets, as they were situated at your time of birth, are placed within the houses and are interpreted according to their position in an astrological sign and house. You will see lines, called aspect lines, linking some of the planets. These are significant mathematical distances between two or more points on your chart, and interpreting them adds extra depth to your birth chart.

The most crucial element to interpreting your chart is learning how to look at the whole picture, instead of merely assessing each component individually. This book takes you through that process step by step, so that you can enter into an exciting journey of self-discovery and then use your skills to interpret the birth charts of the people around you.

5 Only got five minutes?

Astrology is the study of the influence of the planets and constellations on our lives. In order to discover how the heavenly bodies have a personal impact, you will first create a map of the heavens as they looked at the moment of your birth. This is called a birth chart, or natal chart, and can be viewed as a key to the psyche, to your character and disposition. Within your birth chart you can find your likes and dislikes, your special gifts and talents, the areas of life which you find most challenging, and your attitudes towards work, play, socializing, finances, relationships, communication and many other areas of life.

The natal chart is divided into 12 segments. The outer circle shows the position of the constellations at the time of your birth, and the actual moment of birth is defined by the Ascendant, which marks the beginning of the inner 12 segments. These inner sections are called the houses. These describe the different areas of life, and the positions of the planets and asteroids within these reveal a great deal about how you express yourself in each area. Although the planets and asteroids are situated within the inner segments of the houses, their positions within the astrological signs – the constellations – are equally important for interpreting your natal chart.

Here are just some of the principles of astrology that are explained in *Take Control with Astrology*. In the book you will also learn about the triplicities and quadruplicities, ruling planets, and how to discover your self-expression in all areas of your life.

The astrological signs

Also called the 'Sun signs' or 'Star signs', these are the 12 constellations which are positioned around the outer perimeter of your birth chart. Your date of birth determines which sign you were born under, and your astrological sign gives information about your essential nature and way of expressing yourself.

Aries: 21 March to 19 April. Aries is a leader, with much enthusiasm and a tendency to be impetuous.

Taurus: 20 April to 20 May. Taurus is loyal, practical, reliable and determined, with great inner strength.

Gemini: 21 May to 21 June. Gemini is fun-loving, mischievous, communicative, curious and sociable.

Cancer: 22 June to 22 July. Cancer is emotional, sympathetic, caring and can be quite eccentric.

Leo: 23 July to 22 August. Leo is optimistic, positive, generous, creative and has a sense of drama and showmanship.

Virgo: 23 August to 22 September. Virgo is practical, discriminating, helpful and has a desire to be useful.

Libra: 23 September to 22 October. Libra seeks harmony, has a strong sense of fairness and is warm-hearted and loving.

Scorpio: 23 October to 21 November. Scorpio has intense emotions, is introspective, and has strong intuition.

Sagittarius: 22 November to 21 December. Sagittarius is curious, optimistic, energetic, independent and honest.

Capricorn: 22 December to 19 January. Capricorn is responsible, reliable, goal-oriented and practical.

Aquarius: 20 January to 18 February. Aquarius is humanitarian, innovative, unusual and independent.

Pisces: 19 February to 20 March. Pisces is emotional, sensitive, empathetic, gentle and idealistic.

The houses

These are the different areas of your life. Each house is ruled by an astrological sign and one or more planets.

First house: Your outer personality, how others view you.

Second house: Your resources, and inner strength and determination.

Third house: Your ideas, and your manner of learning and communicating.

Fourth house: Your roots and security, and childhood environment.

Fifth house: Your creative impulses, and your sense of play and drama.

Sixth house: Your attitudes towards health and work, and your need to feel useful.

Seventh house: Your relationships and partnerships, and sense of justice.

Eighth house: Your inner strength and endurance, and dealings with others' resources.

Ninth house: Your attitudes towards higher education, travel and abstract thought.

Tenth house: Your goals and ambitions, and your career.

Eleventh house: Your attitudes towards friendships and group activities.

Twelfth house: Your inner-self and unconscious mind, and gifts of compassion.

The planets

The Sun reveals how you express your basic nature and your willpower.

The Moon shows your emotional nature and nurturing tendencies.

Mercury indicates your thinking processes and how you communicate.

Venus shows your attitudes towards love and relationships.

Mars reveals your energy, drive and initiative.

Jupiter shows how you grow and expand as a person.

Saturn indicates how you deal with responsibility.

Uranus indicates where you seek innovation and reform.

Neptune reveals the workings of your imagination and your idealism.

Pluto shows areas in which you experience or seek transformation.

Chiron indicates how you develop wisdom and inner healing.

The aspects

Specific mathematical relationships between the planets are called aspects. When planets are linked in this way it emphasizes the influences of both planets on your personality and attitudes. Understanding these gives you a deeper insight into who you are and why you feel and behave as you do.

Conjunctions: These occur when there are less than ten degrees distance between components in the natal chart. Conjunctions signify action, self-expression and dynamic energy in the areas involved.

Sextiles: These occur when two or more components are situated between 55 and 65 degrees apart. Sextiles add harmony and ease of self-expression to the areas involved.

Squares: These are noted when two components of your chart are placed between 82 and 98 degrees apart. Squares indicate conflict between these areas of your personality, and show where you need to deal with challenges.

Trines: These occur when two components of your chart are situated between 112 and 128 degrees apart. Trines show areas of additional harmony and benefit, and can indicate gifts or talents.

Oppositions: These are found where components of the chart are situated directly opposite each other, between 170 and 180 degrees apart. These, depending on the areas involved, can signify inner-conflict which needs resolving, or special gifts or challenges.

An accurate interpretation of your natal chart involves far more than taking each component piece by piece. You can view each component as part of a jigsaw puzzle, and gradually fit those pieces together to reveal the whole picture of your personality.

In this book you will discover how to synthesize all of the information that you will be studying, and find out how to interpret your birth chart in detail. As an illustration of how the principles work, and to help guide you through this process, film-maker Jen Govey's birth chart will also be interpreted for you section by section.

10 Only got ten minutes?

What is astrology, and why does it work?

Astrology is an ancient art and science which reveals how the planets, asteroids and constellations have a subtle yet profound influence on our lives. The sciences, particularly the New Physics, now teach us that everything in existence takes the form of vibrations and that our universe is a complex web of interconnections. Fundamentally everything in existence, from a nebula to a star, to the atoms within our bodies, are all composed of trace elements which emerged moments after the Big Bang gave birth to the universe. All of life contains within it the stuff of stars. It is therefore hardly surprising that we are hard-wired, at the deepest levels of ourselves, to respond internally to the shifts taking place within the cosmos.

The vibrations, which are the essence of everything, interact with each other, regardless of distance, and can be viewed as a symphony composed of more notes than we can possibly imagine. We each have our own special notes within life's complex symphony, and our responses to everything and everyone around us, and to our own inner promptings, are based on the degree of harmony or disharmony that we feel and experience in every given situation. Our birth charts show clearly what we relate to or shy away from, and reveal why our interactions provoke particular feelings.

The oldest science

The ancients somehow knew all of the above – astrology was the first science. Over 32,000 years ago, cave-dwellers marked out the cycles of the moon on animal bones. The ancient Chaldeans used their calculations of the heavenly bodies to predict wars, floods and eclipses with great accuracy. The awe-inspiring stone monuments such as Stonehenge are now thought to have been remarkable cosmic calendars. Somehow, from the earliest days of humanity, there existed the recognition that we are not separate from the wider cosmos, and that planetary events had an impact on life on Earth.

Cosmic influences

We now know that the moon has an effect on Earth's tides, and on bodies of water which also include the fluid within our cells. Sunspot activity increases during the cycles when Jupiter's orbit exerts a stronger magnetic pull on the seething liquid that flows in the outer layers of the Sun. This, in turn, affects weather systems on our planet, which go on to affect plants and crops and the life-forms which need these in order to survive. Our distant companions have a powerful impact on all life on Earth. Knowing this, we can each celebrate our uniqueness while also recognizing that we are part of the magnificent vast interwoven fabric of life.

Your personal map

At the moment of your birth you added your own singular vibrational note to the cosmic symphony. The form this note takes is immediately recognizable to a student of astrology because it is illustrated by the patterns within the map of your natal chart, and those patterns can be interpreted as your personality traits.

If, as a newborn, you could see vast distances and look at the heavens immediately above us, you would see the positions of the constellations and planets in that moment. Your birth chart is a representation of this.

The components in your natal chart

Within your birth chart you will find the constellations (the zodiac signs) around the periphery, the houses (the areas of life) in the inner circle, and the planets and asteroids (psychological patterns) within the houses and the zodiac signs. There are also the angles to consider. These are the Ascendant (your outer personality) with the Descendant (others' impressions of you) opposite. At the zenith of the chart is the Midheaven (your goals), also called the MC (*Medium Coeli* meaning 'the middle of the heavens'), and opposite this, at the Nadir, also called the IC (*Imum Coeli* meaning 'the bottom of the heavens'), which represents your roots.

Certain mathematical relationships between the planets are called aspects, and these are shown within the birth chart by connecting lines, some of which form patterns that act as extra personality markers.

Each astrological sign and planet is attributed a gender which gives further clues in interpretation. Masculine energy is more dynamic and forceful, whereas feminine energy is quieter and more inward-looking. The signs considered to be masculine are Aries, Gemini, Leo, Libra, Sagittarius and Aquarius. The feminine signs are Taurus, Cancer, Virgo, Scorpio, Capricorn and Pisces. The feminine planets are the Moon and Venus.

The constellations

The constellations in your chart are the 12 signs of the zodiac – the 'Sun signs' or 'Star signs.' The Earth travels the course of the zodiac over the period of a year. The astrological signs are Aries, Taurus, Gemini, Cancer, Leo, Virgo, Libra, Scorpio, Sagittarius, Capricorn, Aquarius and Pisces, and each of these signify particular modes of self-expression, which are further emphasized when planets are found in the signs.

Aries is the sign of willpower, energy, initiative and action.

Taurus is the sign of practicality, planning ability, steadfastness and sensuality.

Gemini is the sign of communication, versatility, curiosity and sociability.

Cancer is the sign of nurturing, vulnerability, emotion and sensitivity.

Leo is the sign of leadership, courage, warmth and creativity.

Virgo is the sign of discrimination, intelligence, orderliness and service to others.

Libra is the sign of justice, balance, harmony and artistry.

Scorpio is the sign of deep-thinking, emotional depth, tenaciousness and willpower.

Sagittarius is the sign of independence, honesty, energy and philosophical thought.

Capricorn is the sign of self-discipline, practicality, goal-orientation and emotional maturity.

Aquarius is the sign of innovativeness, quirkiness, free-thinking and humanitarianism.

Pisces is the sign of sensitivity, compassion, empathy and idealism.

Your date of birth determines which sign the Sun was in when you were born. If your birthday is 1 January, the Sun would have been positioned in the zodiac sign of Capricorn, and this indicates that your basic, essential nature is expressed through practicalities. The Sun in Capricorn would emphasize your gifts of determination and staying power. You may be mature for your age, with a wry sense of humour, and an ability to attain your goals through sheer focus and hard work will make you a valued member of the community. If you were born on 1 June, your Sun is in Gemini, indicating that your basic, essential nature is curious and vivacious. Your special gifts would include those of versatility and communication, and you may be viewed as an interesting and stimulating companion.

Triplicities and quadruplicities

The astrological signs are each associated with a triplicity and quadruplicity, which adds more to your understanding of the birth chart.

The **triplicities** are the four elements: fire, earth, air and water.

- ▶ **Fire** *(Aries, Leo, Sagittarius): This brings energy and motivation, swift decision-making and action.*
- ▶ **Earth** *(Taurus, Virgo, Capricorn): This brings determination, perseverance and reliability.*
- ▶ **Air** *(Gemini, Libra, Aquarius): This brings communication skills, innovative ideas and curiosity.*
- ▶ **Water** *(Cancer, Scorpio, Pisces): This brings emotional resonance, sensitivity and a need for privacy.*

The **quadruplicities** indicate your general approach to life. These are called cardinal, fixed and mutable.

- ▶ **Cardinal** *(Aries, Cancer, Libra, Capricorn): These indicate strong leadership abilities and assertiveness.*
- ▶ **Fixed** *(Taurus, Leo, Scorpio, Aquarius): These indicate goal-orientation, reliability and determination.*

▶ **Mutable** *(Gemini, Virgo, Sagittarius, Pisces): These indicate flexibility, resourcefulness and adaptability.*

The Ascendant and houses

The time of birth determines your Ascendant and the positions of the houses in your chart. The Ascendant marks the moment of birth or, according to some astrologers, the first breath, which signals entry into your new life. The Ascendant is the astrological sign which is rising on the Eastern Horizon, and this, the beginning of the first house of self-expression in your chart, changes at two-hourly intervals as the Earth spins on its axis. Because of this comparatively swift movement, even twins will each have a different degree of Ascendant, and therefore a slight shift in the pattern of the birth chart. Geographical placement also has an effect on the position of the Ascendant, because the heavens look different from London, Sydney and New York.

From the Ascendant, the wheel of the zodiac moves anti-clockwise around the perimeter of your natal chart. The inner circle is divided into the 12 spokes of another wheel – the houses – which represents the areas of your life. The degree of the beginning of your Ascendant – your moment of birth – defines the degree of each house that follows on from it. So with Jen, whose birth chart is interpreted in this book, the Sun was in Leo when she was born, and her Ascendant was Cancer. The positioning of the houses means that Jen's Sun is in the third house. An astrologer would immediately see that Jen's essential nature, Leo, is fun-loving, creative and that she glows when praised. And also that outwardly, through her Ascendant, Jen is rather shy and retiring, and it takes her a while to really let herself shine around people she doesn't know. The Sun in her third house indicates that she enjoys, and is good at, communication, and that she has speaking and writing abilities.

The planets

In astrology the planets are affiliated with archetypes, particular patterns within the psyche which are common to all cultures and are imprinted deep within each of us. We tap into these archetypes while telling stories, because they express human nature and qualities in a way that is larger than life yet identifiable with elements of ourselves. The names of the planets, apart from the luminaries, the Sun and Moon, are derived from Greek and Roman myths, and understanding the characters in the stories can give you a deep insight into the specific personalities and qualities of these mythical beings which makes the planets easier to interpret in your study of astrology. You can explore this, if you wish, in my book *Understanding the Planetary Myths*.

Each of the planets embody qualities in your psychological make-up, and the position of a planet in a sign and house reveals how you express yourself.

The Sun is symbolic of the conscious mind, of self-expression and of the strength of your will. It reveals the light of the inner personality. Enthusiasm, confidence, courage, creativity and growth are also elements of Sun interpretation, and your Sun sign reveals a great deal about your essential nature, even if outwardly you may appear to be governed more by your Ascendant.

The Moon represents the subconscious mind, dreams, deep emotions, and the relationship with the mother and other women. Your desire to nurture is expressed through the position of your Moon.

Mercury reveals how you communicate in speech and writing, how you use your intelligence and what interests you. It gives information about relationships with family, especially siblings, and neighbours. It also indicates your powers of discrimination and decision-making.

Venus shows your attitudes to relationships, your desire for love and how you find ways in which to meet your emotional needs, your perception of and attraction to harmony and beauty, and the creative and artistic impulses which bring you pleasure.

Mars shows your passion and drive, your energy and initiative, and how strongly you feel compelled to carry forward the urge to fulfil your desires. Your physical expression through areas such as sports, is governed by Mars.

Jupiter shows the areas in which you achieve expansion and growth, how you follow your philosophical interests, and indicates your qualities of generosity, benevolence and intellectual thinking that lead you to both mental and physical explorations.

Saturn reveals your gifts of self-discipline and order, and shows how you cope with, and break through, constrictions and limitations. Strong willpower and determination are Saturnian qualities which can help you achieve your goals.

Uranus shows the areas of life where you think outside the box, open yourself to intuition and inspiration, and use your intellectual abilities in unusual, though often scientific, ways. The position of Uranus also shows where you resist constraints and insist on freedom of expression.

Neptune reveals how you experience, express and channel your deepest emotions. Depending on its position in your chart, these emotions may take the form of turbulence and escapism, flights of fancy, or high spiritual insights. Neptune is the planet of idealism and empathy, and can unlock the portal to the intuition and your most profound insights.

Pluto shows you where you use your deepest resources, inner willpower and tenacity in order to regenerate aspects of yourself and/or your life. This is the planet of profound transformation, and enables you to connect with the promptings of your unconscious. Pluto also shows how you deal with external resources.

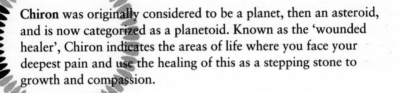

Chiron was originally considered to be a planet, then an asteroid, and is now categorized as a planetoid. Known as the 'wounded healer', Chiron indicates the areas of life where you face your deepest pain and use the healing of this as a stepping stone to growth and compassion.

The aspects

An aspect is a significant mathematical relationship between two or more planets or angles in your birth chart. Depending upon the factors involved, the effect could be easy and harmonious or stressful and challenging. However, the challenging aspects can often be used to develop strength and build character, and are present in the charts of many successful people. There are several *minor* aspects, but in this book we are focusing on the *major* aspects.

Conjunctions: A conjunction occurs when two components in your natal chart are situated within ten degrees of each other. This powerful aspect emphasizes the qualities of both components, and adds dynamism to the qualities expressed by them.

Sextiles: A sextile occurs when two components of your chart are between 55 and 65 degrees apart. This brings additional harmony to the characteristics of both components.

Squares: When two components of your chart are between 82 and 98 degrees apart, you have a square aspect. This adds tension to both components, and indicates issues that will take effort to overcome.

Trines: A trine occurs when two components of your chart are between 112 and 128 degrees apart. Trines add ease of expression and increased harmony, and help you to develop your potential in the areas involved.

Oppositions: When two components are directly opposite each other, 170 to 190 degrees apart, they are said to be 'in opposition'. This can indicate gifts or challenges, and often signifies the presence of inner conflict.

Synthesizing the chart interpretation

Take Control with Astrology shows you how to interpret each component of your natal chart individually and then put the pieces of the puzzle together to form the whole picture.

Introduction

'Who am I? Why am I here? How can I discover and fulfil my potential?' Most people will ask these questions at some point in their life and there is a system that can be used to guide us towards the answers. This is the art of astrology.

Astrology is the study of the constellations and planets, and how these have an effect on our lives. Your birth chart, or natal chart as it is also called, is a map of the heavens at the moment of your birth and is a blueprint of your personality. This contains information about all of the diverse factors that make you the person that you are, with your own particular perception of yourself and of the world. It reveals the gifts and strengths that you can develop and the psychological challenges or weaknesses that you can work on in order to live life in as constructive and empowered a manner as possible.

No two birth charts are ever exactly the same – even twins have slightly different birth charts because there will have been a brief time lapse between the birth of each child. The Ascendant (or rising sign, as it is also called) is the astrological sign that is found on the Eastern Horizon at the time of birth. This changes every two hours, so that even a few minutes' time difference will change the degree of the Ascendant and therefore subtly alter the structure of the birth chart.

The basis for your astrological chart is your time, date and place of birth. The time of birth is extremely important for an accurate birth chart, but if this is not known, astrologers usually create a solar chart in which the Ascendant is placed in the astrological sign in which the Sun is situated. There are ways in which the chart can be made more accurate through narrowing down the time of birth to, for example, lunch-time, and some astrologers also use a pendulum to dowse for the birth time if circumstances such as adoption make it very difficult to find the information that is needed.

Your birth chart can reveal a great deal about your personality. It can help you to understand yourself more fully and can show your potential gifts, the type of challenges that you are likely to have to deal with and your attitudes towards different areas of your life such as relationships, finances, health and career. It is your choice how or whether you develop the potential that is revealed in your birth chart, but using the information in your chart can enable you to understand yourself more deeply, can help you to make the most of opportunities in your life and can be very useful in guiding you to find beneficial avenues of self-expression, which you may not have previously considered.

Types of astrology

There are several ways in which astrology can be used. The focus in this book is that of character analysis, but you may find that you wish to explore other areas of astrology as well.

- *Sun-sign astrology is the most publicized because you can read an interpretation of your daily, weekly or monthly horoscope in many newspapers and magazines. This is generalized because it is structured to conform to one-twelfth of the population and, unless your Sun sign is also the same as the sign on your Ascendant, is less likely to be highly accurate.*
- *Synastry is the use of astrology in order to discover the compatibility of two people and the dynamics within a relationship. The information in both birth charts is put together and reveals how each person relates to the other in all areas of life. Synastry can be useful for romantic relationships, parent–child relationships and business partnerships.*
- *Horary astrology is the calculation of an astrological chart at a precise time, in order to answer a question that is asked at that time.*

- *Electional astrology is also concerned with timing. The astrologer will calculate the most constructive time for planning particular events, using the information in your birth chart and future astrological influences.*
- *Predictive astrology uses the information in your birth chart in comparison with current and future astrological configurations to examine future trends in your life and to guide you in how to make the most of these.*
- *Some astrologers specialize in health or medical astrology, which involves examining health issues and the most effective ways in which you can deal with these.*
- *Another area of specialization is that of financial astrology, which looks at specific financial trends such as the stock market.*
- *Mundane astrology is the study of the influences of the planets on global events, as each country is allocated an astrological sign.*
- *Locational astrology, or astrocartography, uses your birth chart to discover the most propitious places for you to live in order to fulfil your highest potential.*

A brief history of astrology

Although astrology is often viewed as an art, it is in fact the oldest science in the history of humanity and was the forerunner of the first sciences. From ancient cultures worldwide through to medieval times, astrologers were also astronomers and mathematicians. The stars and the planets were used for determining the destiny of the rulers of countries, as guides for plotting courses for travel, for predicting eclipses and wars, and for assessing the best times in which to plant foodstuffs.

The cave dwellers of over 32,000 years ago marked the cycles of the Moon on animal bones. In Mesopotamia 4,000 years ago, the Chaldeans recorded the movements of the planets and constellations to predict floods, eclipses and wars. From Mesopotamia, astrology spread to Ancient Egypt, Greece and Rome, and was used by great thinkers such as the philosophers

Socrates, Ptolemy, Aristotle and, much later, was a source of study for Copernicus and his followers. The Mayan calendar has, for over 3,000 years, been used to predict events according to the stars. The creators of the great stone circles around the world planned their monuments for astrological and astronomical calculations.

Claudius Ptolemy was born in Egypt almost 2,000 years ago and became a Roman citizen. A philosopher and scientist, he wrote the first texts on astrology, a quadripartite, or set of four books, and called it *The Tetrabiblios*.

De Revolutionibus was written in 1530 by the Polish astronomer and mathematician Copernicus, but he held back from publishing it because his then heretical conviction that the Sun, not the Earth, was in the centre of the solar system was certain to bring the wrath of the Church. It was published in 1543, the year of his death. The Italian scientist Giordano Bruno espoused the theories of Copernicus and stepped forward to assert that space spread out to infinity and included other solar systems. Bruno was questioned by the Inquisition and burned at the stake in 1600 for his theories. In 1633, another celebrated Italian scientist, Galileo Galilei, narrowly escaped a sentence of death and was forced to renounce his discoveries and his assertions that Copernicus and Bruno were right in their theories.

In those days, the Church and royal families had personal astrologers and astrology was taught in universities. After the Renaissance, astrology became popular only as a form of personal fortune-telling and its reputation began to decline until the advent of the Theosophists in the nineteenth century, who reintroduced a more in-depth esoteric perspective of astrology. The eminent Swiss psychiatrist Dr Carl G. Jung was an advocate of astrology as a means of self-understanding and wrote widely about it. Bruno and Louise Huber trained with psychologist Roberto Assagioli (who had also been taught by Jung) in Italy and founded the Astrological Psychology Institute in Switzerland and the UK. The emergence of astrology as a valuable psychological tool has been further strengthened through the work of astrologers and authors such as Liz Greene and A. T. Mann.

Chart calculation

Up until recently, birth charts were laboriously calculated and drawn up by hand, and some people still prefer to do this as it can help to increase a feeling of involvement and connection with the personality that the chart is being set up for. However, great accuracy is necessary as a small mistake can alter the resulting information and give an inaccurate birth chart. For manual chart calculation the tools of the trade are an astrological ephemeris for the year of birth, containing the sidereal (star) time for each date, an atlas for the longitude and latitude of the birth place, information on time zones in order to correct the time of birth to Greenwich Mean Time, a table of houses containing logarithms for calculation of the Ascendant and Midheaven, and a ruler and protractor.

The easiest and quickest method of chart calculation is to key the birth data into a computer program, either one that you have bought or one that is already installed on an astrology website. Initially, it is simplest to visit a reliable website in order to have your birth chart calculated. If you then decide that you wish to pursue astrology seriously and set up many birth charts, it can be helpful to install a reputable program on your computer.

All that you need for a computerized birth chart is your time, date and place of birth. All of the calculations are then done for you in a matter of moments and you can save, copy or print your chart for interpretation. Some websites offer computerized charts free of charge, most ask a fee for interpretation. However, a computerized interpretation of your birth chart merely interprets the planets, asteroids, houses and aspects by rote, as individual components, and does not synthesize the information. It is more useful (and interesting) to fully interpret your own birth chart. You can find details of useful websites (for free chart calculation and buying astrology software) and further information in the Taking it further section.

How to use this book

This book will show you how you can interpret your astrological chart in a simple, straightforward manner, which enables you to gain a great deal of insight into your personality. Part one explores the components of the birth chart and gives information about the astrological signs, houses, planets and aspects. Part two takes you through step-by-step chart interpretation. This is broken down into 12 areas of life so that you can easily discover how to develop your gifts and potential and can find constructive ways in which to deal with challenges that may be reflected within your birth chart. A sample astrological chart, that of film-maker Jen Govey, is used as an example throughout, so that you can see how the principles of interpretation work. By the end of this section, the charts shown on page xxxix will make perfect sense! Part three is brief and looks at how astrology can be used alongside other systems of self-understanding and development.

Throughout this book are exercises designed to help you to explore the information in your birth chart. Doing these exercises will enable you to gain perceptions into your personality and you may wish to have a notebook that is used solely for these notes and observations.

A message from Jen Govey

I was absolutely delighted and flattered when Lisa asked if she could use my chart to demonstrate interpretations as a part of *Take Control with Astrology*. I wonder whether it was a particularly nice alignment of the planets that helped it along, or whether it was just a lucky coincidence that I had been delving deeply into my own chart, looking for answers to help with my healing and life journey. I was stuck on a little icon that looked like a key, in Aries in my eleventh house. It was quite strongly aspected with my Sun,

(Contd)

Mercury and Uranus, and I wanted to unlock its secrets. I couldn't find much in my astrology books, so I called my friend Lisa. I always call Lisa in these situations as she has a wondrous abundance of knowledge and, as usual, she came through with flying colours and opened up a whole new meaning to my chart and a deeper understanding of myself.

The key, I discovered, was Chiron, the wounded healer. With Lisa's coaching and additional reading of her previous astrology book, *Understanding the Planetary Myths*, I came to learn more about the psychology and deeper meaning: Chiron reminds us that only through recognizing and accepting our inner wounds can we find true healing. It was one of those 'Eureka' moments. Maybe it was coincidence that Lisa had just been asked to write this book while all this self-discovery was going on, and she was just as fascinated with my chart as I was at that moment in time.

Of course I leaped at the chance of Lisa delving even further into my cosmic closet for the book. The experience has left me a lot more confident about my potential in the film industry. I kind of always knew I was destined, but it's fantastic to find my potential and motivations so detailed in my chart, to see how I can make it work for me and what I need to watch out for. I'm even looking forward to meeting my future man, a prospect I had found totally bewildering before!

Take Control with Astrology is innovative in its presentation of astrology, and its format allows you to understand, in a more practical way, your psychological make-up, how to make the most of your untapped potential and how to overcome your own personal hang-ups and demons. I am so very pleased that you have an opportunity to learn from Lisa's wisdom and experience in *Take Control with Astrology* and I hope you are able to fulfil your own potential through understanding your birth chart.

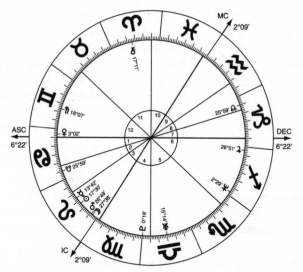

Figure 0.1 Jen's planetary positions.

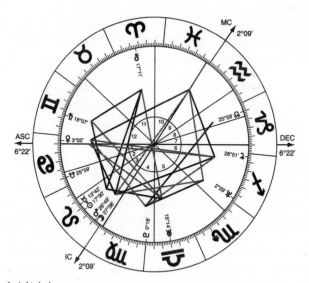

Figure 0.2 Jen's birth chart.

Part one
The basics

1

The components of the natal chart

In this chapter you will learn:
- *about signs, planets, houses, angles and aspects*
- *about the glyphs, the astrological language*
- *about how to interpret your birth chart.*

The astrological signs

These are the 12 constellations, which form patterns in the sky. Each has its own myths and stories that can be traced back to ancient civilizations. The astrological signs, also called the Sun signs, are situated in the outer circle, which forms the rim of the birth chart, and are placed in an anti-clockwise order. Your Sun sign is determined by your date of birth, so you would call yourself an Aries, for example, if you were born during the time period which is allotted to that sign, between the 21 March and 19 April.

The 12 Sun signs are Aries the Ram, Taurus the bull, Gemini the twins, Cancer the crab, Leo the lion, Virgo the virgin, Libra the scales, Scorpio the scorpion, Sagittarius the archer, Capricorn the goat, Aquarius the water bearer and Pisces the fish. Your Sun sign reveals the core of the 'inner you' and the qualities of your essential nature. It gives information about how you express your basic personality and shows the most constructive way in which you can follow your path of personal growth. Each of the Sun signs is ruled by one planet (or sometimes two planets), whose influence has a powerful effect on the sign that it rules. The astrological signs are explored in depth in Chapter 2. Each of the astrological signs, and the planets and aspects that you will find out about later, have their own symbol, called a glyph. These may seem complex or confusing at first, especially as some initially appear to look similar, but you will find that you will learn them easily after starting to explore your birth chart. It may help you to make your own list of these, so that you can familiarize yourself with them more quickly.

THE GLYPHS FOR THE ASTROLOGICAL SIGNS

♈	Aries	♎	Libra
♉	Taurus	♏	Scorpio
♊	Gemini	♐	Sagittarius
♋	Cancer	♑	Capricorn
♌	Leo	♒	Aquarius
♍	Virgo	♓	Pisces

GENDER

The astrological signs are each considered to have a specific gender. This explains the mode of activity for each.

Masculine signs are considered to be more active and aggressive, to be highly motivated and to take initiative. The masculine astrological signs are Aries, Gemini, Leo, Libra, Sagittarius and Aquarius.

Feminine signs are considered to be more introverted, passive and more attuned to their feeling nature. The feminine astrological signs are Taurus, Cancer, Virgo, Scorpio, Capricorn and Pisces.

The main angles of the birth chart

The four main angles within the birth chart (also called the quadrants) are the Ascendant (ASC), Descendant (DEC), Midheaven (MC) and Nadir (IC).

THE ASCENDANT (ASC)

This point in your birth chart marks the moment of birth and the beginning of your life journey and is governed by the astrological sign that is rising (ascending) on the Eastern Horizon at that time. The astrological sign on your Ascendant gives information about how you express yourself outwardly, your approach to life and how others perceive you. The Ascendant is not always the same sign as the astrological sign in which your Sun is situated, as it is calculated from your time of birth and your Sun sign is calculated from your day of birth, but if you were born around sunrise, the Sun sign and Ascendant will be found within the same astrological sign. Unless your Sun sign and Ascendant are the same, your Ascendant may seem to be stronger at times because it represents how you project your personality. However, the Sun-sign qualities of the inner you, though they may not always be to the fore, are an integral part of your nature and are likely to emerge at particular times.

THE DESCENDANT (DEC)

This is found directly opposite your Ascendant. This reveals how you relate to others, shows your approach to relationships and partnerships and also tells you about the impressions that other people have of you.

THE MIDHEAVEN (MC)

MC stands for *Medium Coeli* ('the middle of the heavens'). This is the zenith of your birth chart, the point furthest south (the highest point in the heavens, directly overhead at the time of birth). The MC reveals your public persona and can indicate elements such as fame or notoriety if there is a strong focus on it from planets in your birth chart. Your goals and ambitions, your vocation, hopes and aspirations, and your career are associated with the MC.

THE NADIR (IC)

IC stands for *Imum Coeli* ('the bottom of the heavens'). This is directly opposite the MC and represents the Nadir, the lowest point in the heavens at the time of birth (the point furthest north). The IC represents your roots, your sense of belonging and your need for security. Whereas the MC represents your public personality, the IC is perceived as your private persona.

Insight

The four angles of your birth chart are the Ascendant, the Descendant, the Midheaven (MC) and the Nadir (IC).
The Ascendant and Descendant are found on the same line bisecting your birth chart horizontally. The Midheaven and the Nadir are found on the line which bisects your chart vertically.

The houses

The 12 houses represent the areas of life and divide the circle of the birth chart into segments. The first house begins at the Ascendant, which you will see at the 9 o'clock position on your chart, and the progression, as with the Sun signs, moves anti-clockwise. The astrological sign that is found over each house is determined by the sign that is on the Ascendant, and the combination of house and the astrological sign under which it is situated adds particular qualities to the interpretation of the birth chart. Your Sun sign and Ascendant sign will only be the same if you were born around sunrise.

The houses, in order from first to twelfth, give a great deal of information about your focus in life. These will be explored in more depth in Chapter 3, but, simply put, these govern the areas of self-expression, possessions, communication, the home and family, creativity, work and service to others, partnerships, finances and fundamental psychological patterns and beliefs which are important to you, higher learning, goals and career, social issues and groups, and spirituality and secrets.

There are several different systems for determining the placements of the houses from the Ascendant onwards and we will look at the three main systems that are in use. The oldest method, dating back over 2,000 years, is the Equal House system (see Figure 1.1), where each house is exactly 30 degrees apart, so that the horoscope wheel

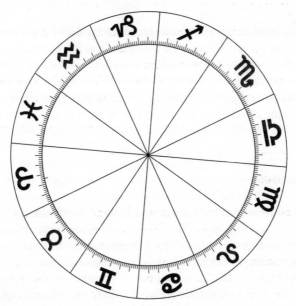

Figure 1.1 The equal house system.

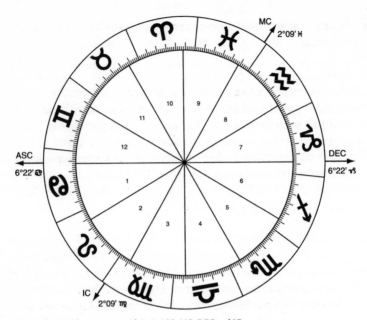

Figure 1.2 The equal house system with Jen's ASC, MC, DEC and IC.

is divided into 12 equal segments from the point of the Ascendant.
This can create confusion with the placement of the Midheaven
(MC), the zenith of the birth chart. The MC is taken to mark the
tenth house, but in the Equal House system may be seen to be
situated in the eighth, ninth, tenth or eleventh houses. As you can
see from the blank chart for Jen's time of birth (Figure 1.2), the
MC would be placed in the eighth house according to this system.

Although the birth chart looks like a flat circle, it actually
represents a three-dimensional sphere, so other house systems
are more representative of this. The Placidus house system was
originated by a monk and mathematician called Placidus de Tito in
the seventeenth century. This is the most popular system today and
is used in *Raphael's Ephemeris* (an annual publication giving the
year's planetary positions) for chart calculation and in Jen's sample
chart throughout the rest of this book. The houses look unequal
because the chart is representative of a three-dimensional sphere.
If you wish, you can experiment with these various systems in

order to discover which feels more comfortable for you to work with.

> **Insight**
> The houses are the 12 segments within your birth chart.
> These are numbered anti-clockwise and represent the areas of
> your life: self-expression, possessions, communication, your
> home and family, creativity, work and health, relationships,
> resources, higher education and travel, your goals and career,
> friendships, and your inner life.

The planets

Planets within a particular house add focus and impetus to the area of life which is governed by that house. If no planets are found within houses in your birth chart, you can still gain information through looking at the sign that is found on the cusp at the beginning of those houses. This is called the overlay.

The heavenly bodies have a powerful influence on our lives and personality. The vast nuclear furnace of the Sun breathes life into our solar system and its gravitational field holds the planets on their orbits around it. The Moon governs the tides on Earth and affects bodies of water, in turn affecting us at a cellular level because our cells are mostly composed of water. And the interaction between the heavenly bodies influences life on Earth. The gravity of Jupiter's orbit affects sunspot cycles. Sunspots were first observed by Galileo in 1610, and look like dots or blemishes on the surface of the Sun. They are bursts of electrical activity which send beams of negatively charged ions into space. Those which enter the Earth's atmosphere create the spectacular visual effects of the Aurora Borealis, increase the amount of ozone in the upper atmosphere which, through increased absorption of heat from the Sun, affects our weather systems, and have a disruptive effect on radio transmissions. Sunspots occur in 11-year cycles, and peak when the orbits of Jupiter and Saturn move across each other and intersect.

The planets are also associated with archetypes, imprinted cross-cultural psychological patterns, which have been explored in myths and stories throughout history. The planets in astrology are named after the deities of Ancient Greece and Rome, and the personalities of those archetypal figures shine strongly through the attributes associated with their planetary counterparts. If you view each of these heavenly bodies as an element within your personality, you can understand and relate to their qualities more easily. This is explored in depth in my book *Understanding the Planetary Myths*. Depending upon the positions of the planets in your birth chart, these facets of yourself can be either constructive or difficult to deal with, and studying your birth chart enables you to find ways in which to integrate the various facets of your personality for maximum growth and self-understanding.

The Sun and Moon are also called the luminaries in astrology. Although the Sun is not a planet, it is interpreted as such and, in the sequence of the planets in chart interpretation, the Moon, our satellite, follows the Sun. Then come Mercury, Venus, Mars, Jupiter, Saturn, Uranus, Neptune and Pluto. Until recently, Pluto, which is smaller than the Earth's moon, was considered to be a planet. It has now been reclassified by astronomers as a 'dwarf planet', though its astrological interpretation is unchanged. Chiron, which was previously considered to be an asteroid but is also classified astronomically as a planetoid, is situated between Saturn and Uranus but, because of its unusual status, is usually interpreted after Pluto.

Each planet has an affinity with one or more astrological signs, as you will see in Part two. The planets are also considered to be what is termed 'exalted', 'in detriment' or 'in fall' in particular signs. This will be indicated in the information given about the astrological signs in Part two. When a planet is 'exalted', as in the Sun in Aries, this means that it expresses its most positive energy in that sign. 'In detriment' means that the planet is situated in the astrological sign opposite its ruling sign. 'In fall' means that the planet's influence is at its lowest in a particular sign. Not every Sun sign has a planet in exaltation or in fall.

GLYPHS FOR THE PLANETS

⊙ The Sun   ♄ Saturn

☽ The Moon   ♅ Uranus

☿ Mercury   ♆ Neptune

♀ Venus   ♇ Pluto

♂ Mars   ⚷ Chiron

♃ Jupiter

> Calculate your birth chart and look at it closely. Note down your Sun sign, Ascendant and in which signs and houses the planets, MC and IC are found. Determine whether there are any signs or houses in your birth chart that contain several planets. If there appears to be a concentration of planets in one astrological sign or house, this will show you where a great deal of your focus lies.

Insight

Each planet is associated with one or more astrological sign and house. The planets reveal the various facets of yourself, and the position of each planet in the signs and houses tells you a great deal about how you feel, think, act and react.

The triplicities

The 12 signs of the zodiac are divided into three groups of the four elements – fire, earth, air and water. The triplicities (see Figure 1.3) reveal your temperament and how you express your personality. If a high proportion of planets are situated in one element, such as

Figure 1.3 The triplicities.

Earth, you will express yourself according to the qualities of Earth
and are likely to take a practical approach to matters in your life.
If you have no planets in another element, such as fire, the qualities
of that element will be dormant – you may find it difficult to
become excited or motivated.

FIRE – ARIES, LEO, SAGITTARIUS
(GENDER: MASCULINE)

The element of fire is excitable, enthusiastic, passionate, dynamic,
creative and forceful. A predominance of fire in your chart indicates
that you are swift to act but do not always pause to think through

the consequences. You have a great deal of energy and motivation, but you tend to burn out or lose enthusiasm quickly.

EARTH – TAURUS, VIRGO, CAPRICORN (GENDER: FEMININE)

The element of earth is practical, dedicated, determined, hard-working and has strong staying power. A predominance of earth in your chart indicates that you are reliable, committed and able to plan in advance, and work steadily to achieve your goals.

AIR – GEMINI, LIBRA, AQUARIUS (GENDER: MASCULINE)

The element of air is curious, communicative, sociable and has a fascination for ideas, change and innovation. A predominance of air in your chart indicates that you need a great deal of social and intellectual stimulation in order to capture your interest, and you enjoy being around other people.

WATER – CANCER, SCORPIO, PISCES (GENDER: FEMININE)

The element of water is emotional, sensitive, intuitive and changeable, with strong feelings and a tendency towards introversion. A predominance of water in your chart indicates that you need to have your own 'space' where you can retreat from cares and concerns. It also indicates that you are strongly affected by atmospheres and the moods of those around you.

The quadruplicities

The 12 zodiac signs are also divided into four groups of three signs, called the quadruplicities (see Figure 1.4). These reveal your approach to life, indicating whether you are especially adaptable, resourceful or spontaneous.

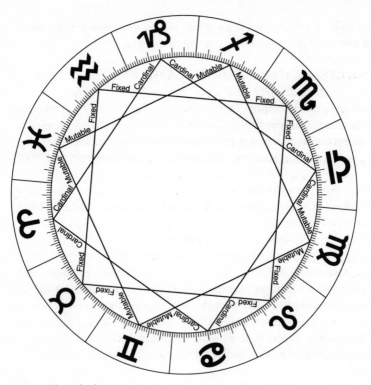

Figure 1.4 The quadruplicities.

CARDINAL – ARIES, CANCER, LIBRA, CAPRICORN

Cardinal signs are determined, strong-willed, assertive, confident and decisive. If you have a predominance of planets in cardinal signs in your chart, you have strong leadership qualities, are good at organizing and making decisions and have abilities to find creative solutions to problems.

FIXED – TAURUS, LEO, SCORPIO, AQUARIUS

Fixed signs are reliable, determined, predictable and tend to have fixed opinions. If you have a predominance of planets in fixed signs you are a hard worker, with a goal in sight that you aim towards unerringly. You are good at planning and have strong powers of endurance and perseverance.

MUTABLE – GEMINI, VIRGO, SAGITTARIUS, PISCES

Mutable signs are helpful, flexible, resourceful and enjoy change. If you have a predominance of planets in mutable signs, you prefer to co-operate with others and tend to want the best for everyone. You are good at adapting to new situations.

Count the triplicities and quadruplicities in your birth chart. Which of each of these contains the most planets? This tells you how you approach life and respond to situations.

Insight

The triplicities are the elements of fire, earth, air and water found in your birth chart, and reveal information about your temperament and self-expression. The quadruplicities are divided into cardinal, fixed and mutable, and indicate your approach to life. Each of the astrological signs is associated with a triplicity and quadruplicity.

The Moon's nodes

The Moon's nodes are not heavenly bodies, but are points in the birth chart where the path of the Moon intersects the path of the Sun. There are two nodes, the north and south, and these are also called, respectively, the Dragon's head and the Dragon's tail. They are placed directly opposite each other in the birth chart. The astrological sign and house in which the Moon's nodes are found give information about how you express yourself.

The North node ☊☊ reveals how you deal with prevailing trends within your society and culture, and how you connect or fit in with this. The North node also reveals your sense of timing – whether you are able to make decisions that correspond with what is needed or acceptable at the time. Astrologers view the North node as being an indicator of the good karma that you have earned, the principle of reaping what you have sown.

The South node ☋ reveals the character traits, habits and tendencies that have been created through your reactions and responses to past experiences. Often these are expressed unconsciously and can result in habits or patterns of behaviour that are not constructive to your sense of well-being.

The aspects

An aspect is a significant mathematical distance between two planets or angles in the birth chart. This reveals specific areas of harmony or stress that arise when two heavenly bodies are in relationship to each other. You could view an aspect as two elements of the personality which either work well together or create conflict. The planets that are in aspect to each other and the signs and houses in which they are situated are interpreted in order to give a deep insight into your gifts and challenges, and can even reveal why you are the way you are.

There are major and minor aspects in astrology, but we will focus only on the major aspects in this book. These are called conjunctions, sextiles, squares, trines and oppositions. If you calculate a birth chart manually, you would need to use a protractor to discover which of the planets are in aspect to each other. If you have your chart drawn up using a computer program, the aspects will already be calculated for you. They are shown in boxes along with your birth chart. Each aspect has an acceptable distance that is allowed beyond the exact point of connection. This is called an orb. When you interpret the aspects, consider the nature of the aspect and the characteristics of the planets in aspect to each other. Look at which signs and houses are involved. This enables you to gauge the effect of the aspect on your personality and areas of your life.

The aspects are shown in two forms in your birth-chart data: as lines within the birth chart (see Figure 1.5) and in a grid (see Figure 1.6). The grid makes it easy to see at a glance which aspects exist between the planets and angles. If you calculate a chart manually, you would fill in this grid first and then use that information to draw the aspect lines on the chart itself. On a computerized chart, you will receive a grid and the lines on your birth chart will also be drawn automatically for you. The lines for the sextiles and trines are usually drawn in grey and the lines for the squares and oppositions are drawn in black. As the conjunctions are very close together, there is not really any need to mark these with a line.

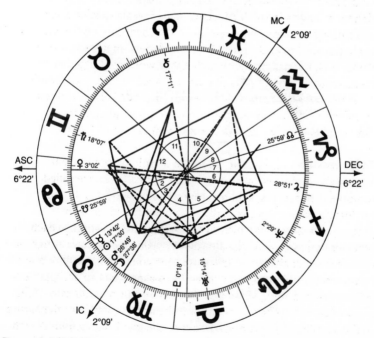

Figure 1.5 Jen's birth chart.

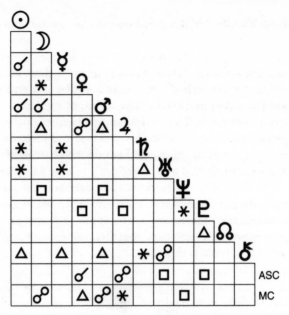

Figure 1.6 Jen's aspect grid.

THE GLYPHS FOR THE MAJOR ASPECTS

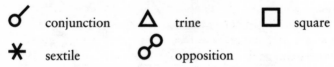

☌ conjunction   △ trine   □ square

✶ sextile   ☍ opposition

THE CONJUNCTION (ORB 10 DEGREES)

This aspect occurs when two planets (or a planet and chart angle) are situated very close together, between 0 degrees and 10 degrees apart. A conjunction is a powerful aspect because it brings two components of your birth chart and your personality into a close, strong relationship. This can be viewed as positive or negative, depending upon the planets involved and whether they interact harmoniously or discordantly. The qualities of the conjunction are action, dynamism, self-expression and transformation.

THE SEXTILE (ORB 5 DEGREES)

A sextile spans a distance of one-sixth of the birth chart. It occurs when two planets, or a planet and chart angle, are 60 degrees apart with a 5 degree orb allowed on either side. A sextile is a harmonious aspect and brings out the positive side of both factors concerned. The quality of the sextile is ease of self-expression.

THE SQUARE (ORB 8 DEGREES)

A square spans a distance of one-quarter of the birth chart. It occurs when two planets, or a planet and chart angle, are 90 degrees apart with an 8 degree orb allowed on either side. A square indicates conflict between the qualities of the two factors involved and within your personality. This reflects areas of your life where you have to strive to overcome challenges or obstacles, and it can be difficult to deal with, but square aspects can help to create inner strength.

THE TRINE (ORB 8 DEGREES)

A trine spans one-third of the birth chart. It occurs when two planets, or a planet and chart angle, are 120 degrees apart with an 8 degree orb allowed on either side. A trine is a powerfully harmonious aspect and reveals areas where potential can easily be developed and goals can be accomplished. It brings ease of self-expression, the development of gifts or talents and a positive approach to life.

THE OPPOSITION (ORB 10 DEGREES)

An opposition spans one-half of the birth chart. It occurs when two planets, or a planet and chart angle, are 180 degrees apart with a 10 degree orb allowed on either side. The Ascendant and Descendant, the MC and IC, and the Moon's nodes are each naturally in opposition to each other, as they each bisect the birth chart. The opposition can reveal either gifts or challenges, depending upon the factors involved, but generally is interpreted as a need for resolution of an inner or outer conflict.

Aspect patterns

Aspects between the planets, asteroids and angles are shown in your birth chart as lines within the inner circle of your chart. If you look carefully at these, you will see that patterns emerge. Some astrologers interpret the overall pattern of the aspect lines as being a reflection of your spiritual quest or development. However, even without considering this, you can discover a great deal about yourself from merely looking at how the planets and the aspect patterns are placed.

Insight
The aspects are significant mathematical relationships between two or more components of your birth chart. These show areas of particular harmony, talents, gifts or challenges in the areas of life where an aspect is situated. The aspects are called conjunctions, sextiles, squares, trines and oppositions.

If you have a predominance of planets in close quarters, this indicates that you have a strong focus in that particular area. If the planets are scattered around your chart, this reveals that you tend to scatter your energy widely and may have many interests but find it hard to focus. Planets that are spaced equally on both sides of your chart, in a see-saw shape, indicate that you shift easily from one side of your personality or manner of expression to the other. A semi-circle of planets, like a bowl, with one side of your chart left empty, reveals that you scoop up experience in order to use it. A triangle shape reveals strong focus, with the apex of the triangle being your goal.

A grand trine occurs when three planets are placed at an equal distance of 120 degrees, in trine aspect to each other. This is viewed as bringing a great deal of harmony to the personality, but it can mean that life is so easy that you don't have as many opportunities to grow through facing challenges.

A grand cross is found when four planets are situated with 90 degrees between planets. This reveals that there are powerful challenges to be dealt with and creates stress and tension. However, the charts of many highly successful people contain a grand cross, because the determination to overcome challenges forges strength and determination.

Look at the pattern that the aspects make in your chart. What image does this conjure up in your mind and what does this remind you of? This tells you whether your focus is concentrated, scattered, or whether you prefer to look for balance and weigh up possibilities. Consider whether there is a predominance of particular aspects; whether you have mostly conjunctions, sextiles, squares, trines or oppositions. If so, this will tell you how you perceive your life – whether you feel that life is generally easy and straightforward, or whether you feel that you are frequently struggling. When you interpret your chart in depth later on, you will discover how to use this information constructively.

Interpreting the birth chart

Firstly, study the meanings of the glyphs, as these are surprisingly easy to learn. Initially you will need to keep referring to these, so you may wish to make a note of all the glyphs on a separate piece of paper, and keep this beside you until you have familiarized yourself with their meanings.

To interpret your birth chart systematically, you begin with the positions of the Sun, Moon and Ascendant. Your basic, essential nature is revealed through your Sun sign and the house in which it is found. Your inner emotional nature is revealed in the sign and house where the Moon is situated. The Ascendant informs you about how you express your personality outwardly and how other people perceive you. Look at the placement of the Midheaven for your goals, ambitions, hopes and dreams. Consider the number of planets in each gender so that you can see whether your chart shows you to be active and an initiator or more passive and sympathetic. Count the number of planets, asteroids and angles in the triplicities and quadruplicities, and take note of the signs and houses in which these are situated. Look then at the aspect pattern to gauge your main mode of self-expression.

Mentally divide the chart into two sections: above and below the Ascendant. Planets in the top part of the chart show that you are outgoing and interactive. A predominance of planets in the lower half of your chart reveals that you are more introspective.

You can then interpret each planet in its sign and house, followed by aspects between the planets. You may find that some information appears to conflict until you look closer and see how the different parts of your personality fit together. As some planetary placements are stronger than others, you will soon learn to distinguish which are more dominant. If there are no planets in a sign or house, this indicates that the qualities of this sign or house are not being utilized or developed. However, in this case, you can gain additional insight by looking at the positions of the ruling planets of those sections of your chart, and interpreting these in the context of the area of life which you are exploring. In Part two of this book, you will look at how this can be used to understand how you respond, act and react in the various areas of your life.

Also in Part two, you will discover how to divide the information in your chart into specific areas of your life, to gain an immediate assessment of the astrological information about how you express yourself, seek security, communicate, find meaningful work, relate to others and so on.

10 THINGS TO REMEMBER

1 *Your birth chart is a map of the heavens at your moment of birth.*

2 *Your chart is calculated by your date and time of birth.*

3 *The time of year when you were born determines your Sun sign.*

4 *Your time and place of birth determines your Ascendant.*

5 *The Midheaven reveals your goals and aims.*

6 *There are 12 astrological signs and 12 houses.*

7 *Your Sun sign describes your essential nature.*

8 *Your Ascendant reveals how others see you.*

9 *The houses represent the areas of life.*

10 *The planets reveal your psychological patterns and responses.*

2

The Sun signs

In this chapter you will learn:
- *about the astrological signs*
- *about their ruling planets, triplicities and quadruplicities*
- *about how these impact on your relationships and career.*

> **Insight**
>
> The fire signs represent action and initiative, enthusiasm,
> leadership qualities and impulsiveness. If you have a
> predominance of fire in your natal chart you will tend to be
> quick-thinking and acting, full of ideas, but may have a low
> boredom threshold.

Aries

21 March–19 April
Gender: male
Planetary rulers: Mars and Pluto
Triplicity: fire
Quadruplicity: cardinal
Exalted: the Sun
In detriment: Venus
In fall: Saturn

Aries is symbolized by the ram, a headstrong creature with
abundant energy and willpower. This is the sign of action

and initiative, of leadership and innovation. Arians are confident, impetuous, quick-thinking and fast acting, with a fascination for all that is new and untried. Unexplored territory is appealing to you because this gives you the opportunity to put your own mark on it and learn something new in the process. You are enthusiastic and motivated by the prospect of adventure. You need challenges to pit your wits against and are good at finding unusual solutions to problems. However, although you are good at initiating new ideas and projects, you prefer to have other people take over the mundane side of matters, as you grow bored easily. Thoughts and emotions are always close to the surface – you walk your talk as long as your interest is held; when your interest wanes you swiftly move on.

You tend to act without thinking things through first and you feel driven to follow your impulses. This can create awkward situations or misunderstandings because sometimes, in your haste to move forward, you forget to consider the feelings of others. You are keenly competitive and like to be 'first' in everything as you have a strong drive to prove yourself.

The ruling planets are Mars and Pluto. Mars brings action and dynamism and a quick temper. Pluto brings an intensity of feeling and a need to be in control.

LOVE AND CAREER

As an energetic Aries, you need to feel excited and stimulated by the people around you. You're a romantic and are attracted to those who share your enthusiasm for adventure. The other fire signs, Leo and Sagittarius, spark off your romantic and passionate streak. Consider which qualities in other signs would appeal to you. Your career needs to be stimulating with plenty of scope for change or you will swiftly become bored. Coaching, law, couriering, sales or PR work could provide the diversity you need.

Keywords: energetic, impetuous, headstrong, leadership qualities, enthusiastic.

The earth signs represent staying power, practical, logical
thinking processes, determination and goal-orientation.
If you have a predominance of earth in your natal chart
you will tend to be reliable and trustworthy, dedicated
and hard-working.

Taurus

20 April–20 May
Gender: feminine
Planetary ruler: Venus
Triplicity: earth
Quadruplicity: fixed
Exalted: the Moon
In detriment: Mars

Taurus is symbolized by the bull, a creature renowned for its
powers of strength and endurance. Like the bull, you are
generally easy-going and slow to anger but, if goaded, you
become a force of nature that can only be stopped when
you have used up your available energy. You prefer to
work your way steadily through life, applying yourself to
achieving long-term goals and to surrounding yourself with
comforts and all the luxury you can accumulate. To you,
possessions are important because these help you to feel secure
emotionally as well as physically. Security is paramount for
Taureans.

The senses are your avenues of expression. Appealing fragrances,
stirring music, fabrics that feel good to the touch, beautiful
surroundings and belongings, and the delights of good food all
nourish your spirit. Beauty is vital to your well-being and you
take care to ensure that your surroundings are as opulent and
harmonious as your finances permit.

You can be intensely possessive of people as well as possessions and your underlying fear of losing what you have makes you hold on tightly to what you perceive is yours. As a fixed sign, you can be extremely stubborn if others oppose you. You take your time to come to decisions and you cannot be persuaded to act unless you have thought through all angles of the matter at hand. You are a master at planning, with good business sense, and are capable of working steadily towards long-range goals. Commitment and loyalty are your bywords and you expect others to be as committed as you are, whether this is within a romantic relationship or business partnership.

LOVE AND CAREER

As a steadfast Taurean, you look for a romantic partner who will share your love of food and the good things in life, and who will be tactile and supportive. The other earth signs, Virgo and Capricorn, understand your need for security. Consider which qualities in other signs would appeal to you.

Your career is viewed as a long-term commitment and you are prepared to undergo lengthy training if necessary. Your talent for finances can be useful for banking or advisory work, and your keen senses could be well employed within the catering or beauty industries, or the arts.

Keywords: practical, sensual, loyal, stubborn, possessive, reliable.

Insight
The air signs represent ideas, communication, and the ability to welcome in the new and untried. If you have mainly air in your birth chart you will tend to enjoy socializing and exchanging ideas with other people.

Gemini

21 May–21 June
Gender: masculine
Ruler: Mercury
Triplicity: air
Quadruplicity: mutable
In detriment: Jupiter

Gemini is symbolized by the twins, which illustrate the dual nature of this astrological sign. Your realm is that of communication and information and your curiosity is boundless. You have a quick mind and are immensely adaptable, tending to flit swiftly from one idea or train of thought to the next, even though your companions may not recognize any connection between these. You thrive on stimulation, whether this comes through learning a new skill, taking part in interesting conversations or rushing off to pursue whatever captures your interest at that moment.

Mercury, your ruling planet, is the messenger of the zodiac but is also a mischief-maker. You have an innate sense of fun and can be entertaining and amusing company because of your quick-wittedness, but you also find it hard to resist the temptation to gossip and poke fun at others. You are easily bored and are likely to be a jack of all trades, learning a little about every subject that appeals to you but losing interest if deeper study is involved. This ability to grasp the essentials of many subjects can make you appear more knowledgeable than you really are. Repartee is one of your skills and you always have a quick and often amusing response to comments from others. Your easy sociability and ability to blend, chameleon-like, into any group of people makes you popular and you are likely to have a wide range of different types of friends.

LOVE AND CAREER

As a Gemini, you gravitate towards romantic partners who are also friends, and stimulating conversation is important to you. The other air signs, Libra and Aquarius, share your need for communication and for broadening your intellectual horizons. Consider which qualities in other signs would also appeal to you.

You may switch careers several times until you find something that holds your attention. Information is important to you so a career in the media would suit you. Writing, sales, driving or translating would also provide the diversity you need.

Keywords: communication, sociable, mischievous, fun-loving, adaptable.

Insight

The water signs represent emotion, sensitivity, compassion and intuition. If you have a predominance of water in your natal chart you will tend to be guided by your feelings, and may be changeable according to your moods. You will also be highly sensitive to the moods of others.

Cancer

22 June–22 July
Gender: feminine
Ruling planet: the Moon
Triplicity: water
Quadruplicity: cardinal
Exalted: Jupiter
In detriment: Saturn
In fall: Mars

Cancer is symbolized by the crab, which aptly describes your soft, vulnerable centre hidden within a protective outer shell. You are emotional and retiring, highly sensitive to atmospheres and the moods of others, and can be grouchy if challenged or offended. Although you are shy until you feel able to trust those around you, you have an off-beat sense of humour and a kind, caring nature. Security is vital to your well-being and you find it deeply painful if you are not accepted, foibles and all, by the people whom you care about.

You are the nurturer of the zodiac and willingly bring others into your protective sphere if they are in need of a mother-figure, regardless of your gender. The home is your domain and you use your innate creativity to make this a place of comfort and emotional warmth. Cancerians are renowned for being good cooks and you view cooking as a way in which to nurture those around you.

Your sensitivity enables you to empathize with others, but this can make you feel overwhelmed if you are not able to retreat to your personal space in order to recharge yourself. This sensitivity can work against you as you are quick to take offence, even if it is not intended, and you can retaliate harshly and then withdraw when you are upset. Like the changeable Moon, your ruling planet, you are prone to mood swings and this can confuse those around you. You are possessive and, although you balk at emotional pressure from others, you do not hesitate to use it yourself in order to achieve your aims. You prefer to follow your own path, even if this entails walking to a different rhythm from everyone else. Yet, when your sympathy is aroused, you will sacrifice anything for your loved ones.

LOVE AND CAREER

The Cancerian fear of rejection can make it difficult for you to make the first move in romance, but once committed, you are loyal and devoted. You easily gravitate towards the other water signs, Scorpio and Pisces, as they share your deep emotional nature. Consider which qualities in other signs would also appeal to you.

The ideal work environment is one where you can care for others. Cooking, the medical profession, mentoring, farming or agriculture, history or archaeology are likely to appeal to you.

Keywords: sensitive, nurturing, sympathetic, eccentric, moody, possessive.

Leo

23 July–22 August
Gender: masculine
Ruling planet: the Sun
Triplicity: fire
Quadruplicity: fixed
In detriment: Saturn

Leo is the sign of the lion and aptly illustrates the leonine qualities of courage, leadership and pride in accomplishments. You carry yourself with a bearing that could be termed regal and, like your ruler the Sun, your leadership qualities, warmth and strength of personality attract others to bask in the benevolent glow of your presence. You love to be surrounded by admirers and are at your best when you are the centre of attention. Compliments or praise give you the confidence to express the best side of yourself, although this does make you susceptible to flattery and hangers-on. Criticism crushes you and you find it hard to pull yourself back up if you are denigrated or harshly treated.

You are immensely creative and have a sense of drama that brings flair to your activities and endeavours. To you, the world is your stage and you thrive on applause. You are willing to give a great deal of your time and attention to those in your inner circle and are generous to a fault, but your interest drops away if you feel ignored or slighted or if your pride is offended.

Details are boring to you and you prefer to let others deal with those as you look at the overall picture. This can trip you up at times and you need to share your ideas and projects with those whom you trust to take care of the nitty-gritty, which you find uninteresting but which can ensure your success.

You are a romantic and tend to fall in love easily, especially if the recipient of your attraction is willing to follow your lead.

Creative people interest you as they spark your own creativity, and you have a strong sense of form and beauty.

LOVE AND CAREER

As a Leo, you are a true romantic and need to feel cherished yet emotionally and mentally stimulated. The other fire signs, Aries and Sagittarius, suit your passionate nature. Consider which qualities in other signs would also appeal to you.

A career in the arts or drama is likely to appeal to you. Designing clothes or jewellery allows you to express your creative side, and teaching would suit your love of children and your sociable nature.

Keywords: positive, benevolent, creative, dramatic, romantic, generous.

Virgo

23 August–22 September
Gender: feminine
Ruling planet: Mercury
Triplicity: earth
Quadruplicity: mutable
In detriment: Jupiter

Virgo is the sign of the Virgin, who carries the wheatsheaf of grain that symbolizes the harvesting of experience and the ability to sort the wheat from the chaff. Discrimination is one of your keywords and you use your intelligence to sift ideas in order to decide what will be useful and productive. Your ruler, Mercury, gives you a keen mind and acute perception and in Virgo is used in a more serious light than in fun-loving Gemini, which Mercury also rules. Virgoans often have an air of purity and wholesomeness.

Practicality is important to you and you enjoy being useful to others. This is the sign of service. It lights up your day if you have made someone feel happy or good about themselves. This can lead to you feeling overburdened at times, as you will give all of yourself until you feel exhausted and then rebel and insist on having your own space until you have regrouped your reserves of energy.

Details fascinate you and you tend to forget that there is a larger picture. You are orderly, and it can upset you to the point of being detrimental to your health if you are surrounded by chaos. This does not mean that all Virgoans are scrupulously tidy, but you can usually instantly pinpoint where anything is that you need. You have a highly developed critical faculty and, at your worst, can be nit-picking, though you judge yourself even more harshly than you judge others and become distressed if you are not living up to your high standards.

Health and nutrition are immensely interesting to you and you are likely to be an advocate of complimentary therapies and healthy living. Stress can give rise to nervous and physical complaints, and can adversely affect your delicate digestive system.

LOVE AND CAREER

You are discriminating in your choice of romantic partners and would rather be single than with someone incompatible. The other earth signs, Taurus and Capricorn, understand your practical nature. Consider which qualities in other signs would also appeal to you.

Careers in the health or dietary areas would suit you as these allow you to help others as well as satisfying your interests. Writing or journalism, or secretarial or PA work allow you to use your attention to detail.

Keywords: discriminating, calm, critical, practical, productive, helpful.

Libra

23 September–22 October
Gender: masculine
Ruler: Venus
Triplicity: air
Quadruplicity: cardinal
Exalted: Saturn
In detriment: Mars
In fall: the Sun

Libra is the sign of the scales of justice and balance – and, to you, fairness is a major issue. Your ruling planet, Venus, bestows a sense of beauty and harmony and adds a romantic appeal to your personality. You are gentle and sweet-natured, eager to please those around you and your warmth, charm and sociability ensure that you have a wide circle of friends and admirers. However, if you encounter injustice, in any form, you transform into a warrior in defence of what is right and tend to champion those who do not have someone to argue their case. You are loyal and your ability to listen often puts you in a position of confidante or counsellor.

Artistic, musical and creative, you thrive when you can express your gifts and talents, and respond best to kindness and encouragement. Harsh words and coarse attitudes upset and offend you. Your sense of beauty extends to many areas and you take pride in good clothes and pleasing decor.

Because you tend to see both sides of any situation, it can take you a long time to come to decisions. You weigh up and measure everything inwardly and this can make you appear to be indecisive. Once your mind is made up, however, you act on your decisions.

People fascinate you and you enjoy interacting with a wide range of personalities as you need intellectual stimulation. You are intensely romantic and thrive on the feeling of partnership within a relationship, although for you to be truly happy this needs to be one where you are an equal partner.

LOVE AND CAREER

The Libran tendency to fall in love easily makes you susceptible to displays of affection. Your need for communication, friendship and romance makes the other air signs, Gemini and Aquarius, compatible. Consider which qualities in other signs would also appeal to you.

Your intelligence and sense of justice makes legal or mediation work an ideal career. Your artistic nature and sense of beauty is compatible with the arts, music, and the beauty or design industries.

Keywords: gentle, harmonious, intellectual, creative, fair, sociable.

Scorpio

23 October–21 November
Gender: feminine
Ruling planets: Pluto and Mars
Triplicity: water
Quadruplicity: fixed
In detriment: Venus
In fall: the Moon

Scorpio is symbolized by the scorpion, a creature which prefers to quietly go about its own business but whose sting in its tail can be lethal when it is threatened. The eagle, with its ability to soar high above the landscape and see every detail clearly, is also a symbol of Scorpio. Your primary ruling planet, Pluto, is the mythological ruler of the Underworld, the home of the dead and of the Earth's treasures. You are a deep thinker, strongly intuitive, and you take life seriously. Often there is an interest in death and the afterlife, as you strive to understand life's mysteries. You have tremendous tenacity and powers of endurance and your strong willpower, a gift from both Pluto and Mars, enables you to soldier on against all odds in order to achieve your goals. The fixed nature of Scorpio makes you stubborn and capable of tremendous perseverance.

Your emotions are powerfully felt and you are willing to give your all if you feel that others deserve your support. However, if you are offended, you will either strike out or walk away, determined never again to have dealings with that person. You have high expectations of yourself and others and a deep-rooted need to be in control. This can make you manipulative as you easily perceive people's strengths and weaknesses.

The aura of mystique that surrounds you is attractive to others, and your ability to penetrate beyond the usual boundaries can be either intimidating or fascinating. You are courageous, perceptive and do not suffer fools gladly. Outspoken if your opinion is asked, you prefer to remain silent and to observe others in order to decipher the root of any matter that engages you.

LOVE AND CAREER

As a Scorpio, your intensely emotional, passionate nature is most easily understood by the other water signs, Cancer and Pisces. Consider which qualities in other signs would also appeal to you.

Your investigative abilities make any career that allows you to track down information appealing, so work as an investigator, psychologist or psychiatrist if possible. Your enjoyment of danger yet need for privacy may open doors as a stunt person or security guard. A career in finance would also suit you.

Keywords: powerful, persevering, deep-thinking, emotional, intuitive.

Sagittarius

22 November–21 December
Gender: masculine
Ruler: Jupiter
Triplicity: fire
Quadruplicity: mutable
In detriment: Mercury

Sagittarius is embodied by the centaur, Chiron – half-man, half-horse – with his bow and arrow poised, aiming at its target. This represents the pursuit of knowledge as Chiron was the mentor and teacher in the Greek pantheon and your symbol immediately points out your profound intellectual capabilities, idealism, boundless curiosity and desire to be of help. You are energetic, enthusiastic, determined to learn and to pass on what you know to others. Jupiter's rulership bestows a positive, optimistic attitude and the conviction that your opinions are worth paying heed to.

You are impetuous and tend to jump to conclusions, but your keen intellect constantly spurs you on to accumulate understanding. You tend to be conventional and traditional in your attitudes, even though you prefer to think of yourself as a free spirit and you dislike being pinned down. Independence is vital to your well-being. Your easy-going nature and fascination with the thoughts and opinions of others bring a wide social circle and you thrive on the realm of ideas. Outspoken and truthful, you can inadvertently cause offence by voicing your opinions without considering how these will affect those around you, but you are not malicious and are crestfallen if you discover that you have hurt someone's feelings.

The areas of philosophy, education and religion are likely to be of particular interest to you and you revel in bringing abstract ideas into concrete form. You can be a crusader and like to convert others to adopt your points of view. Extrovert and immensely sociable, you have an aura of bonhomie that is greatly appealing to others.

LOVE AND CAREER

As a Sagittarian, you need freedom in relationships, and communication and the bond of friendship are important. The other fire signs, Aries and Leo, spark your sense of adventure and romance. Consider which qualities in other signs would also appeal to you.

Academic work would suit you, especially if this involves teaching or lecturing. A career in religion or philosophy would allow you to explore your interest in these. Your sense of adventure may be directed into sports.

Keywords: enthusiastic, intelligent, outspoken, independent, energetic.

Capricorn

22 December–19 January
Gender: feminine
Ruling planet: Saturn
Triplicity: earth
Quadruplicity: cardinal
Exalted: Mars
In detriment: the Moon
In fall: Jupiter

Capricorn is symbolized by the sure-footed mountain goat, which illustrates your ability to keep your feet on the ground and your sights set unerringly on your goal. Your ruling planet, Saturn, bestows inner strength, pragmatism, practicality and determination, and speeds you into maturity at an early age. You are clear-headed, responsible and a hard worker with workaholic tendencies, always determined to do your best. You are a stringent taskmaster as you expect others to share your sense of commitment, but you are fair with those around you, especially if they stick to the rules which you live by. You can be stubborn and inflexible when crossed, but your serious outer demeanour hides a wry wit and an off-centre sense of humour that may surprise those around you.

You are ambitious and self-disciplined and you set your sights high. No sacrifice is too great in order for you to accomplish your goals, and you make long-range plans and stick resolutely to these. You prefer to keep any worries or anxieties to yourself and you can be prone to depression and fears if you do not allow yourself time for relaxation. If you make a promise, you ensure that it is kept, and you expect others to share your high values.

Structure is important to you. You respect those who are methodical and who, like you, see matters through to their conclusion. With your earthy nature and loyalty you are a steadfast friend and are likely to be respected and relied on by your colleagues.

LOVE AND CAREER

Your Capricorn reserve is overcome by your sense of connection with others who are determined, practical and straightforward, so the other earth signs, Taurus and Virgo, enable you to lower your emotional barriers. Consider which qualities in other signs would also appeal to you.

Your organizational skills fit you for a career in business, financial work, mathematics, science, dentistry or computer programming. Your physical endurance could be useful in sports such as mountaineering.

Keywords: practical, disciplined, ambitious, reliable, responsible, mature.

Aquarius

20 January–18 February
Gender: masculine
Ruling planet: Uranus
Triplicity: air
Quadruplicity: fixed
In detriment: the Sun

The symbol for Aquarius is the water-bearer, pouring life-giving and cleansing water onto the land. This represents your desire to use your life in order to make a difference to humanity. You are independent yet sociable, idealistic, intellectual and a free-thinker, and you tend to relate to groups of people who share a common aim rather than wishing to be pinned down in what you perceive as the stifling atmosphere of close intimate relationships. Even when you are the centre of attention, you exude an air of aloofness and detachment and your mind is always toying with new ideas and concepts, which can sometimes make you appear distracted.

You have an unusual mind, with the ability to go off at tangents and find angles and perspectives that others may miss, and your ruling planet, Uranus, makes you prone to sudden insights and lightning bolts of inspiration and perception. The sciences and technology interest you and you are likely to have a fondness for gadgets. You gravitate towards people who share your love of unusual ideas and you are innovative and at times appealingly eccentric. Your humanitarian qualities make you an active campaigner and you may be perceived as rebellious as you enjoy shifting the status quo.

As a fixed air sign you are drawn to the realm of ideas and can be inflexible in your opinions once these are strongly formed. Yet you enjoy change and may seek this for the sake of learning something new.

LOVE AND CAREER

As an Aquarian, you need to feel that there is a strong friendship within a romance, and have a desire for independence and freedom to follow your own interests. The other air signs, Gemini and Libra, provide the intellectual stimulation you require. Consider which qualities in other signs would also appeal to you.

Your humanitarian qualities make human and animal rights issues possible career choices. The sciences, mathematics, astrology, aviation or electrical and technological work would also appeal to you.

Keywords: humanitarian, sociable, innovative, intelligent, extraordinary.

Pisces

19 February–20 March
Gender: feminine
Ruling planets: Neptune and Jupiter
Triplicity: water
Quadruplicity: mutable
Exalted: Venus
In detriment: Mercury

Pisces is symbolized by two fish swimming in opposite directions. This reveals your tendency to be constantly pulled by the tides of your emotions, and also signifies your ability to connect strongly with the watery element of your own and others' deep feelings. You are sympathetic and empathetic, easily moved to tears of joy or sorrow and you have a deep-rooted urge to take care of those around you. You can be a conundrum as you also need to feel that you are being taken care of and you veer between fragility and strength. Your idealism means that you trust easily and this opens you up to emotional hurts and betrayals, but your gentle, compassionate nature cannot resist a person in need. When hurt you tend to display an emotional outburst and then withdraw, but demonstrations of kindness from others soon lift your spirits again. At times you may feel that the world rests heavy on your shoulders as your sympathy extends to strangers, even those in faraway countries.

You have a vivid imagination and an aptitude for the arts, music and dance, which have a profoundly healing and uplifting effect on you. Neptune bestows visionary qualities and the image-making faculties of your mind are highly developed, while Jupiter gives you the optimism that all will be well. You are mystical in a spiritual rather than religious way and you feel a need to escape from harsh realities. Your creativity is a positive outlet for this as it gives you an opportunity to touch others in a deep and meaningful manner.

LOVE AND CAREER

Your gentle Piscean nature hides a passionate emotional interior and you naturally gravitate towards the other water signs, Cancerians and Scorpios, who understand your predisposition for the emotional heights and depths. Consider which qualities in other signs would also appeal to you.

Artistic and creative careers are well suited to you. Music, dancing, acting, writing and illustrating are good outlets for your creative energy. Counselling and spiritual teaching would enable you to express your compassionate nature.

Keywords: emotional, sensitive, imaginative, gentle, idealistic, mystical.

Insight

Each planet is associated with one or more of the astrological signs, and emphasizes the characteristics and qualities of the sign that the planet holds rulership of. For instance, Mars, the planet of energy and initiative, rules Aries, the sign of leadership and action.

10 THINGS TO REMEMBER

1 *Your Sun sign has a powerful effect on your personality.*

2 *Each astrological sign has a gender which adds to the expression of that sign.*

3 *Every Sun sign is governed by one or more planets.*

4 *The triplicities are the elements of fire, earth, air and water.*

5 *The quadruplicities are called cardinal, fixed and mutable.*

6 *When a planet is exalted, it enables its highest expression.*

7 *When a planet is in detriment its influence is weakened.*

8 *Your Sun sign and Ascendant are not necessarily the same sign.*

9 *Your astrological sign can give clues as to how you approach relationships.*

10 *Your astrological sign contains qualities which can be helpful in your career.*

3

The houses

In this chapter you will learn:
- *the ruling signs and planets of each house*
- *the area of life that each house represents*
- *what this can tell you about your self-expression.*

> **Insight**
> The first house is ruled by Aries, the first sign, and links
> self-expression to Arian motivation. Taurus and the second
> house both govern resources. Gemini and the third house
> relate to communication. If you think of one word to
> describe each house, you can match this description to
> the ruling sign.

The 12 houses are the segments inside the wheel of your birth
chart. Each house governs an area of your life and is ruled by
an astrological sign and a planet, occasionally two planets. As with
the astrological signs, the houses are placed anti-clockwise around
the chart. The first house begins at the point of the Ascendant,
which marks the moment of your birth. As you discovered in
Chapter 1, there are several systems that can be used to calculate
the position of each house in your chart. Throughout this book
we will be using the Placidus system, which gives a high degree
of accuracy.

Insight

The first house begins at the Ascendant, and the houses flow
anti-clockwise around the inner circle of your birth chart.
Their main interpretation is as the areas of life, but some
systems of astrology also use the houses as the chronological
time-line of your life, with planets marking significant events.

It would be helpful to have your birth chart beside you while you
explore what the houses can tell you about yourself. When you
read about the planets in the next chapter, you will be able to
interpret your chart in even more depth, but you can gain a great
deal of information about yourself by considering the qualities
of the natural ruler of each house and exploring these alongside
the astrological sign with its element, triplicity and quadruplicity,
which is found on each house in your chart. Unless your Ascendant
is situated at the beginning of an astrological sign, you will find
that it looks as if there are two astrological signs in some houses.
The one that you should interpret is the sign at the beginning of
each house, but if the sign beside it takes up most of the space in
the house, consider the characteristics of both signs.

Insight

The Ascendant describes the face that you show to the world,
and reveals how you express yourself outwardly. Your
attitude to life, your energy levels and your general motivation
is revealed through your Ascendant and first house.

First house

Ruling sign: Aries
Ruling planets: Mars and Pluto

The first house describes your attitude to life and your outward
personality. This is the part of yourself that others notice first,
before getting to know the deeper layers of your personality.

Your energy and drive, extroverted or introverted approach, your general health and your motivation are all shown in your first house. This house can also reveal information about your early environment. Your Sun sign describes your inner self and your essential nature, but the characteristics of your Ascendant show the face that you present to the world.

As Aries – the ruler of the first house – is governed by Mars and Pluto, this reveals how you act and how you follow your impulses and desires.

Look at the sign on your Ascendant, which governs your first house. The characteristics of this sign will be expressed through your outer personality. This is how others will view you.

Keywords: outer personality, self-expression, energy, drive.

Second house

Ruling sign: Taurus
Ruling planet: Venus

The second house describes your attitude towards resources, both inner resources of strength and outer, material resources. The way in which you view and deal with money and possessions can be seen here, and this house shows how you use these in order to create a sense of security and stability. Your need or desire for comfort and luxury, your attitude towards food and your five senses are governed by this house. The rulership of Taurus and Venus can be experienced through talents such as art or music or through a practical, hands-on approach to tasks.

The association with Taurus gives clues to your inner strength and determination, and your ability to take your time and plan ahead.

Look at the sign that is situated on your second house. See what this tells you about your approach to resources, possessions and talents.

Keywords: resources, possessions, money, talents.

Third house

Ruling sign: Gemini
Ruling planet: Mercury

The third house deals with your manner of communication, your thought processes, speech and writing, curiosity and how you express your ideas. This house represents the practical aspect of your mind and concrete thoughts, whereas the ninth house describes your approach towards more abstract thinking. Your day-to-day communication and relationships with siblings and neighbours can be seen in the third house. Short journeys for work or pleasure can also be indicated here if there are planets in this house. This house can give information about your early education.

The rulership of Gemini and Mercury makes the third house an indicator of your sociability and interest in finding out about the world around you.

Look at the sign on your third house. What does this tell you about your interests and how you communicate?

Keywords: communication, close relationships, speech, education.

Fourth house

Ruling sign: Cancer
Ruling planet: the Moon

The fourth house begins at the IC in the Placidus house system and reveals what you view as the foundation in your life. Your home and family, your relationship with your parents and specifically your mother, and your sense of roots and belonging can be found here. Your childhood environment, and psychological patterns which were set up during your early years, is described in this house. Your own approach towards nurturing and parenting can be found in the fourth house, along with your interest in domesticity and need for a space to call your own. Your sense of history and particular interests in family trees, archaeology or ancestors can be explored here.

The natural rulers of the fourth house, Cancer and the Moon, indicate how you express your emotions.

Look at the astrological sign on your fourth house. Relate the qualities of that sign to your emotional self-expression and your nurturing abilities.

Keywords: immediate family, parents, nurturing, emotions, foundation in life.

Fifth house

Ruling sign: Leo
Ruling planet: the Sun

The fifth house reveals your creative impulses, the extrovert side of your nature and your sense of drama. Planets in this house disclose the medium through which you allow yourself to really shine. Your approach to play, recreation and entertainment, your romantic tendencies and your desire or need for attention are found in this house. Talents in the arts or drama are shown here. Another aspect of the fifth house is your interaction with children, and teaching abilities can be disclosed if you have planets in this house.

The natural rulers of the fifth house, Leo and the Sun, relate to your sense of showmanship and your feelings of goodwill towards those around you.

Look at the astrological sign on your fifth house. What do the qualities of this sign tell you about your sense of play and how you express your creative abilities?

Keywords: creativity, drama, entertainment, arts, children.

Sixth house

Ruling sign: Virgo
Ruling planet: Mercury

The sixth house shows your attitudes towards work and health and also shows how you express your caring nature through being helpful to others. Your ability to focus on details and to discriminate is revealed through the astrological sign and any planets in this house. Here you can discover what influences your approach to grooming, your dress sense and your attitudes towards tidiness and order.

The natural rulers of this house, Virgo and Mercury, indicate how you express your need to make yourself feel useful and valued.

Look at the astrological sign situated on your sixth house. This can reveal what the issues of work, health and service mean to you.

Keywords: work, health, service, discrimination, critical faculties.

Seventh house

Ruling sign: Libra
Ruling planet: Venus

The seventh house begins at the Descendant, directly opposite the point of the Ascendant, and governs relationships and partnerships. Here you can discover your approach towards and need for love and partnership. Marriage and professional partnerships are both indicated here through the astrological sign on this house and any planets within it. The seventh house also relates to how you deal with the general public and shows your sociability and urge for meaningful connection with others. Your underlying sense of justice and desire for fairness for all, and any possible legal issues can be found here if there are planets in this house. Talents in the arts or music are expressed through the seventh house.

The natural rulers of this house, Libra and Venus, denote your sense of beauty and urge for harmony.

Look at the astrological sign on your seventh house.
This can reveal how important relationships are to your sense of self and also any artistic or musical gifts.

Keywords: relationships, partnerships, marriage, love, beauty, justice, artistry.

Eighth house

Ruling sign: Scorpio
Ruling planets: Pluto and Mars

The eighth house governs how you deal with the resources of others, such as wills, inheritances, taxes and corporate finance.

Planets in this house can indicate that money will come your way through the avenue of other people. There is also another aspect to the interpretation of this house. It deals with your powers of regeneration, your inner strength and endurance, and your desire to delve deep below the surface and discover the underlying factors of what is most important to you. The big questions about life and death are examined through the forum of the astrological sign on this house and planets found within it. Your ability to look beyond surface appearances and pierce the veil of illusion is an attribute of this house. Your relationship with the shadowy elements within yourself and your sexual drives can also be deciphered here.

The natural rulers of this house, Scorpio, Pluto and Mars, forge a link with the deep aspects of yourself.

Look at the astrological sign on your eighth house. What do the characteristics of that sign tell you about what is most meaningful to you?

Keywords: finance, tax, inheritance, deep questions, death, sex.

Ninth house

Ruling sign: Sagittarius
Ruling planet: Jupiter

The ninth house reveals your approach towards knowledge, further education and the need or desire to pass on to others all that you have learned. The astrological sign on this house and planets within it give information about how you use the faculty of abstract thought. Issues of higher education or of training and study, which increases your knowledge and understanding of the world and its inhabitants, are revealed in the ninth house. Philosophical thought, interests in religion, law, publishing or teaching are indicated here. This reveals your curiosity about what lies further afield and planets in this house often mean long-distance travel.

The natural rulers of this house, Sagittarius and Jupiter, contribute towards your urge to explore both your internal nature and the outside world and enable you to find ways through which you can expand your mind.

> Look at the astrological sign on your ninth house. Consider how the qualities of this sign are used to enable you to find ways in which to expand your horizons and understanding.
>
> Keywords: higher education, philosophical thought, teaching, expansion.

Tenth house

Ruling sign: Capricorn
Ruling planet: Saturn

The tenth house begins at the Midheaven (MC) in the Placidus system and concerns your career and your public image. Your goals and aspirations, your aims, your drive for success and recognition and your determination to achieve are all found in this house. Planets within this house can indicate high attainment, celebrity or notoriety, depending upon the aspects, and the sign on this house shows you what your attitude and approach is towards fulfilling your goals. High-profile careers, and interests such as politics, are also governed by the tenth house. It shows how you deal with power structures, either as an employer or employee, and marks out your attitudes towards maintaining the status quo.

The natural rulers of this house, Capricorn and Saturn, influence your qualities of perseverance and staying power.

Look at the astrological sign on your tenth house. How can you use the qualities of that sign in order to further your goals?

Keywords: career, ambition, goals, authority, recognition.

Insight

The Midheaven (MC) marks the beginning of the tenth house. This is the area which reveals your ambitions and goals, your career, and any possibilities of public recognition. The Nadir (IC) marks the beginning of the fourth house, and shows your roots, your home life, and your sense of security.

Eleventh house

Ruling sign: Aquarius
Ruling planets: Uranus and Saturn

The eleventh house reveals how you express your ideals and humanitarian impulses within group situations. Your interaction with groups of people, whether this is in a social setting to pursue interests or hobbies or on a more global scale, can be seen in the astrological sign on this house and any planets found within it. Your sense of commitment and responsibility to others, your loyalties and your intellectual, rather than material, goals can be explored through the eleventh house.

The natural rulers of the eleventh house, Aquarius, Uranus and Saturn, influence your ability to follow your chosen path in life through gaining insights into yourself and the world around you.

Look at the astrological sign on your eleventh house. Consider how you can use the qualities of that sign in order to fulfil your higher aims and connect with kindred spirits.

Keywords: group endeavours, sociability, insight, humanitarian principles.

Twelfth house

Ruling sign: Pisces
Ruling planets: Neptune and Jupiter

The twelfth house governs the unconscious mind and influences your dreams, fantasies, tendency towards keeping secrets and your sense of spiritual connection. Whereas the seventh house can reveal open enemies, hidden enemies come under the domain of the twelfth house. Compassion, altruism, the ability to visualize, and artistic gifts that arise through a sense of connection with a source of spiritual nourishment are found in this house. Any escapist tendencies, dependency on alcohol or drugs, institutions, or involvement in spurious undertakings are also revealed in the twelfth house.

The natural rulers of the twelfth house, Pisces, Neptune and Jupiter, influence the ways through which you access the subconscious mind, and find paths to follow, which lead you to an understanding of your inner self.

Look at the astrological sign on your twelfth house. What do the qualities of this sign tell you about how you subconsciously deal with issues in your life and how you express your inner nature?

Keywords: compassion, wisdom, escapism, secrets, spirituality.

Insight

Each house naturally progresses into the next. Self-expression brings the desire for belongings, then interaction with others, which fosters inner security, and which relaxes you enough to play and create. This leads towards thinking of others, and guides you towards relationships, transformation, journeying, focusing on goals, sharing, and caring.

10 THINGS TO REMEMBER

1 *There are 12 houses, each representing an area of your life.*

2 *Each of the houses is governed by an astrological sign and one or more planets.*

3 *The Ascendant marks the beginning of the first house.*

4 *The degree of the beginning of each house cusp is determined by the degree of the Ascendant.*

5 *There are several systems for calculating the degrees of the house cusps.*

6 *The sign to interpret for each house is the sign found at the beginning of the house cusp.*

7 *The sign on each house informs you of the qualities you express through each area of life.*

8 *Your house signs can indicate strengths and weaknesses in specific areas.*

9 *If a house contains planets this reveals how you express yourself in that area.*

10 *If a house contains no planets this can indicate that extra focus is needed.*

4

The planets

In this chapter you will learn:
- *about the ruling sign and house of each planet*
- *about how the planets reveal your personality*
- *about the meaning of positive and challenging planetary aspects.*

Insight

Each planet gives you information about particular facets of your psyche and personality. The sign that a planet is situated in tells you how you express that aspect of yourself. The house position reveals the area of life in which that part of your personality is most strongly expressed or focused.

In your birth chart, the astrological signs that contain planets reveal the qualities within your personality that you express most powerfully. The planets inform you of the various facets that are contained within your psyche and the ways in which you find avenues through which to express these. So, for instance, the sign in which the Sun is found reveals how you direct your will and pursue your path towards personal growth, and the house in which it is found tells you in which area of your life these influences are most strongly felt. Venus shows how you seek to fulfil your need for love and a sense of connection with other people. Mars reveals how you assert yourself. Pluto shows how you express the inner need to be in control of certain areas of your life. We all contain these facets within us and find our own ways through which to find outlets, and your birth chart reveals how you express these different areas of your personality and seek to fulfil your inner needs and desires.

Many astrologers include asteroids in their chart interpretation. In this book, Chiron, which is a planetoid, is included but if you wish to explore the asteroids there are a number of specialist books available.

You may find it helpful to have your birth chart beside you while exploring the planets. You can look at the position of each planet in your own chart as you read about it and gain a much deeper perspective on your personality and self-expression. Even if there are no planets in a house, you can learn a great deal through looking at the position of the planet(s) which rule the sign on that house and relating this to the area that you are exploring.

The Sun

Ruling sign: Leo
Ruling house: fifth

The Sun reveals how you express your inner essential nature and the ways through which you seek to consciously develop your will. The astrological sign in which the Sun is found gives information about how you seek to fulfil your potential and grow as a person. The house in which your Sun is situated reveals the area of life in which you express the qualities of confidence, self-expression, growth and creativity.

If you have more than one planet situated in your Sun sign, you will express the qualities of that sign strongly, through both your Sun and through the modes of expression governed by other planets in that area. If you have no other planets in the same sign as your Sun, you may find that your outward expression relates more to the characteristics of your Ascendant, but your inner nature and self-expression will still relate strongly to the sign in which your Sun is placed. The qualities of each Sun sign are given in Chapter 3.

Positive aspects to the Sun indicate enthusiasm, powerful self-expression and a positive approach to life, confidence, a healthy ego, creative thinking and expression, and robust health. Challenging aspects reveal either lack of confidence or an inflated ego, depending upon the planets and houses involved, and can indicate difficulties in self-expression and tendencies to over-dramatize.

> Look at the area of your birth chart in which your Sun is situated. Are there any other planets present in the same sign? If these are also in the same house as your Sun and do not overlap into the next house cusp, this will add extra strength to all of the heavenly bodies concerned.
>
> Keywords: inner nature, potential, self-expression, growth.

The Moon

Ruling sign: Cancer
Ruling house: fourth

The position of the Moon gives information about how you express your emotional nature. Your innermost feelings, your intuition, your dream life, memory and imagination are all part of the Moon's domain. The Moon governs your instinctive nature and, through its association with the mother, it also reveals your tendencies towards nurturing. Because the Moon affects the tides and bodies of water on Earth, this planet influences the menstrual cycle and fertility. Your domestic skills are revealed by your Moon position, which shows talents in cooking and home-making.

The sign in which the Moon is situated reveals your conditioned emotional responses, habit patterns and relationships with your mother, with women in general and with children. The house in which the Moon is placed reveals the area of life in which you express your emotions most powerfully. Your reactions to others, your sensitivity and your 'gut feelings' are felt most strongly in the area governed by that house.

Positive aspects to the Moon enable you to express your emotions constructively and to access your nurturing abilities. These bring about a strong, reliable intuition and a healthy connection between the conscious and subconscious minds. Challenging aspects reveal comfort-eating, difficulties in emotional self-expression, moodiness or a tendency to withdraw from emotional involvement.

Look at the astrological sign and house in which your Moon is situated. What does this tell you about how you respond and react emotionally?

Keywords: emotions, instinct, intuition, dreams, nurturing.

Mercury

Ruling signs: Gemini and Virgo
Ruling houses: third and sixth

Mercury governs your thinking processes and all forms of communication. This planet reveals how you accumulate, utilize and convey information. Mercury is always found close to the Sun so will be in either the same astrological sign or in the closest Sun sign. Your perception, speech, writing, education, sociability and curiosity all come under the domain of Mercury. Relationships with siblings and neighbours, and short-distance travel are ruled by Mercury.

The astrological sign in which Mercury is situated shows how you express and use your intelligence and your communication skills. The house which Mercury is in reveals the area of life in which you put these skills to effect.

Positive aspects to Mercury bring intelligence, logic, clear communication, and strong powers of discrimination and deduction. Swift-thinking and decision-making, and the ability to learn quickly and effectively are Mercury's gifts. Challenging aspects to Mercury can bring about gossip-mongering, deceit and learning difficulties such as dyslexia or poor concentration.

Look at the astrological sign and house in which Mercury is situated. What does this tell you about how you use your mental faculties, and about how you communicate?

Keywords: communication, discrimination, intelligence, education, curiosity.

Venus

Ruling signs: Taurus and Libra
Ruling houses: second and seventh

Whereas the Moon reveals your inner emotional life, Venus shows how you feel and express your emotions in relationship to others. Venus is the connective force in your birth chart and indicates your needs and desires which relate to love, harmony and artistry. Your sense of beauty, your ability to feel and express love, your desire for communion with the people who are dear to you and the type of people to whom you are romantically and creatively attracted are all within the domain of Venus. Talents in the arts and music can be found through the position of Venus and also of Neptune.

The astrological sign in which Venus is situated informs you about how you express your emotional needs and how you set about fulfilling these, as well as revealing the focus for your sense of beauty and harmony. The house in which Venus is found shows the areas of life through which you channel your emotions, romantic impulses and artistic tendencies.

Positive aspects to Venus indicate a heightened sense of connection with others, an innate charm that attracts others to you, and reveal that your romantic or creative life is likely to bring fulfilment. Challenging aspects to Venus can mean disappointments in love, promiscuity or difficulties in feeling close to other people, and over-indulgence in your spending habits.

> Look at the astrological sign and house in which Venus is situated. What does this tell you about how you connect with others emotionally and how you fulfil your emotional needs?
>
> Keywords: love, connection, harmony, beauty, artistry.

Mars

Ruling signs: Aries and Scorpio
Ruling houses: first and eighth

Mars reveals your energy, drive and initiative, your physical strength and health, and your motivational and leadership qualities. Action and reaction, passion, impatience, aggression and determination are the modes of expression for this planet. Mars represents the desire principle, and its position in your birth chart reveals how you focus on what you want and seek to achieve your aims. Aptitudes for physical activity and sports are revealed through the placement of Mars.

The astrological sign in which Mars is situated reveals how you use your energy and how you follow your urges to take action. The house in which Mars is found shows the area of life in which you thrust yourself forward in a forceful manner.

Positive aspects to Mars indicate a strong physical constitution, bravery and courage in action, immense motivation and a constructive use of aggressive energy. Challenging aspects can reveal a quick temper, aggression, scattered energy and accident-proneness.

Look at the astrological sign and house in which Mars is situated. What does this tell you about how you use your energy in order to fulfil your goals?

Keywords: action, energy, courage, impatience, aggression, sports.

Jupiter

Ruling signs: Sagittarius and Pisces
Ruling houses: ninth and twelfth

Jupiter, the largest of the planets, reveals how you accomplish growth and expansion. Its domain encompasses optimism, benevolence, generosity, higher education, abstract thought, religion and philosophy. A well-placed Jupiter can reveal a broad mind and generous nature and may indicate wealth, as the expansion that this planet rules is physical as well as mental. Jupiter also rules long-distance travel, usually for the purpose of broadening your mental as well as physical horizons.

Jupiter in the astrological signs shows how you express your intelligence and your approach to expanding your mind through abstract thinking and higher education. The sign in which Jupiter is placed reveals how you seek to fulfil your potential for growth and how you use your goodwill towards those around you. The house in which Jupiter is placed shows the area of life through which you actively seek expansion.

Positive aspects to Jupiter indicate cheerful optimism, generosity, bonhomie, high intelligence, a co-operative, spiritual or philosophical attitude, altruism and a desire for knowledge. These may show the potential for wealth and will indicate an enjoyment of the good things in life. Challenging aspects can indicate over-extravagance and over-indulgence and an unrealistic, idealistic approach.

> Look at the astrological sign and house in which Jupiter is situated. What does this tell you about how you can expand and grow as a person?
>
> Keywords: growth, expansion, optimism, higher education, abstract thought, travel, wealth.

Saturn

Ruling sign: Capricorn
Ruling house: tenth

Saturn is the teacher in the zodiac, embodying the lessons that lead to a sense of responsibility and maturity. Self-discipline, determination, staying power, the ability to carry out a task or decision through to its conclusion, and sheer hard work and commitment are the qualities of this planet. Your ability to deal with serious issues and your level of ambition are embodied by Saturn. This planet's 28-year cycle around the Sun gives rise to 'Saturn's return', a period when Saturn returns to its original position on your birth chart. This is viewed as a challenging time as any issues that have not been dealt with are likely to rise to the surface so that you can learn the lessons of responsibility.

Saturn in the astrological signs reveals your approach to commitment, responsibility and how you go about achieving your goals and ambitions. It can reveal what limitations you struggle to overcome and will show how you utilize the qualities of self-discipline and tenacity. Saturn in the houses indicates the area of life in which you take on responsibility or have it thrust upon you, and shows how you manifest self-control and erect boundaries that help you to feel secure.

Positive aspects to Saturn indicate great determination, resilience and powers of endurance and the ability to take responsibility for your life and often also the lives of others. Ambitions are likely to be achieved through perseverance and hard work. Challenging aspects can indicate emotional blockages, insecurity, tendencies towards depression and a feeling that you are engaged in an uphill struggle to attain your goals.

Look at the astrological sign and house in which Saturn is situated. What does this tell you about how you express the qualities of self-discipline, responsibility and the urge to attain your goals?

Keywords: responsibility, maturity, discipline, limitation, ambition.

Uranus

Ruling sign: Aquarius
Ruling house: eleventh

Uranus reveals your urge towards independence and freedom and the paths through which you seek to reform bring about dramatic change and explore innovative ideas. Uranus rules erratic behaviour and eccentric tendencies, and the area of your chart in which this planet is found reveals where you dislike being pinned down or subjected to rules and regulations. The gifts of Uranus are sudden insights and intuitions, which can bring about a powerful change in your perceptions, immense creativity and profound humanitarian instincts and impulses. Electricity, magnetism and technology are ruled by Uranus.

The astrological sign in which Uranus is found will be common to your generation as the planet moves slowly, taking around seven years to pass through each Sun sign. This will indicate how you innovatively create and respond to important changes that are taking place in your immediate sphere, social group and in society as a whole. The house in which Uranus is situated describes the area through which you express your individuality, need for freedom, insight and intuition. Talents in the arts, especially those connected with technology, can also be revealed through the house placement. Friendships and group activities are governed by the placement of Uranus.

Positive aspects to Uranus indicate a sharp, innovative mind and keen intuition, an ability to connect with others and humanitarian tendencies. A strong Uranus can indicate that you are especially gifted in the arts, sciences or mathematics and are perceived as unusual in some way. Challenging aspects to Uranus can denote eccentricity for the sake of being 'different', rebelliousness and an air of detachment which sets you apart from others.

Look at the astrological sign and house in which Uranus is situated. What does this tell you about the changes brought about by your generation and how you use your intuition and ability to discover new ways of thinking and being?

Keywords: independence, humanitarianism, eccentricity, innovation.

Neptune

Ruling sign: Pisces
Ruling house: twelfth

Neptune reveals the more nebulous, mysterious elements of yourself. Intuition, imagination, dreams, artistic impulses, compassion, empathy and the urge to seek a connection with a spiritual source are the qualities of this planet. Neptune shows where you express the mystical elements of your nature and highlights any attraction towards glamour. As it rules the image-making faculty of the mind, Neptune is often prominent in the birth charts of film-makers and actors as well as artists, poets and musicians. When the creative element of Neptune is blocked, it can result in escapism in the form of fantasy, day-dreaming and addictions.

Neptune is a slow-moving planet and takes around 13 years to move through each Sun sign. Like Uranus, it affects the generation in which you are born. Its influence in the astrological sign is felt through the domains of spirituality, art and fashions in imagery and the media. The house in which Neptune is situated reveals the area in which you feel a desire for connection with the deepest parts of yourself. Your dreams and fantasies, your compassion and sympathy, your artistic impulses, dreams and intuitions can be understood through Neptune's position.

Positive aspects to Neptune indicate sensitivity, an artistic temperament and a deep compassion, which brings about a desire to help those less fortunate than yourself. Challenging aspects can give information about tendencies towards escapism, a desire to retreat from the world, involvement with nefarious cults or over-use of drugs, sex or alcohol.

Look at the astrological sign and house in which Neptune is situated. What does this tell you about artistic or spiritual changes that are being brought about by your generation?

How do you express your desire for a sense of connection with others?

Keywords: imagination, intuition, compassion, empathy, escapism, art.

Pluto

Ruling signs: Aries and Scorpio
Ruling houses: first and eighth

Pluto is the transformer and reveals how you both create and react to far-reaching changes in your life. 'Out with the old and in with the new' could be the motto of this planet, as it indicates the forums in which major shifts in your life and consciousness take place. The attributes of Pluto include immense willpower, tenacity, the ability to transform yourself through the situations you find yourself in, and a connection with the deep unconscious mind which spurs you to seek out answers to life's most mysterious questions. Life and death, sexuality, creation, destruction and renewal, and secrecy are Pluto's domain and its position in your chart reveals how you approach and deal with these issues.

In the astrological signs, Pluto influences the generation into which you are born. Its erratic orbit around the Sun takes 248 years, and it spends between 12 and 32 years in each Sun sign. The planet's association with atomic energy is related to its discovery at the onset of the atomic age in 1930. Powerful changes within society are marked through Pluto's passing, and wars and natural disasters such as earthquakes, volcanic eruptions and tidal waves are connected to Pluto. The house in which Pluto is situated reveals the area in which you experience potent change and transformation that leads to increased wisdom, though not always through taking an easy path forwards.

Positive aspects to Pluto indicate tremendous inner resources of strength and endurance, and the ability to cope with far-reaching changes and their repercussions. As wealth is another of Pluto's attributes, positive aspects can indicate financial gain through the resources of others, such as wills and inheritance. Challenging aspects test your inner resources and force you to make changes in areas that you would prefer to remain the same. These aspects can also pinpoint obsessive behaviour and control issues.

Look at the astrological sign and house in which Pluto is situated. What does this tell you about how you express your inner power and the areas in your life which most challenge you to bring about transformation?

Keywords: transformation, willpower, control, inner resources, secrecy.

Insight

These significant relationships between two or more planets add emphasis to the qualities of the planets, and to the sign and house in which the planets in aspect are placed. Some aspects, such as squares, can indicate tension or challenges, while others, such as trines, show balance and harmony.

Chiron

In the debate over the rulerships of Chiron, the top contenders are Virgo and Sagittarius: Virgo because of the element of healing and service to others, and Sagittarius because Chiron was a Centaur and the mentor to both deities and humans in the mythology.

Ruling signs: Virgo and Sagittarius
Ruling houses: sixth and ninth

Chiron is also known as the 'wounded healer'. The area of the chart in which Chiron is found reveals the nature of, and manner in which you find, healing of a deep-seated wound, which has usually been inflicted inadvertently, often in the early years. The insights that you gain from facing and overcoming obstacles are then used to help others around you. The attributes of Chiron include self-empowerment, wisdom and mentoring. Your ability to unearth and heal any deep-seated patterns that derive from past experiences enables you to become more whole in yourself and to develop compassion towards others.

The astrological sign in which Chiron is situated reveals the approach and methods that you can use to stimulate healing. Chiron's house position indicates the area of life in which you experience your inner sense of disempowerment and through which you can work to overcome this. Your desire and ability to help those around you can also be determined here.

Positive aspects to Chiron indicate a constructive approach to overcoming challenges and obstacles, and the development of wisdom, which is used for the good of others. Challenging aspects point out areas in which you attempt to hide from or negate sadness or emotional damage, which has been created through past experiences.

Look at the astrological sign and house in which Chiron is situated. What does this tell you about how you deal with inner pain or sadness, and which areas in your life are most subject to past influences?

Keywords: inner wound, healing, past traumas, self-empowerment, wisdom.

Insight

Asteroids are chunks of rock traveling within the asteroid belt situated between Mars and Jupiter in our solar system. Many of these are used for interpretation in some systems of astrology. Until recently Chiron was considered to be an asteroid, but has now been categorized as a planetoid – a small planet.

10 THINGS TO REMEMBER

1   *The astrological signs containing planets further emphasize your personality traits.*

2   *The planets reveal how you express the facets of your personality.*

3   *Your inner needs and desires are revealed through your planetary positions.*

4   *Planets within a house add focus to that area of your life.*

5   *If a house contains no planets, you may need to explore that side of life in more depth.*

6   *With houses containing no planets, look at their ruling planetary positions.*

7   *Each planet rules an astrological sign.*

8   *Each planet governs the house corresponding with its ruling astrological sign.*

9   *If you have more than one planet in a sign or house, this indicates your energy is strongly focused in that area of self-expression.*

10 *Each planet is associated with a Greek or Roman deity.*

5

··

The aspects

In this chapter you will learn:
- *about the nature of the major aspects*
- *about what these mean in your birth chart*
- *about how you can use the aspects to guide your growth.*

A description of what the aspects are and how they work is
given in Chapter 1. When you interpret the aspects in your birth
chart, you should consider the two planets that are in relationship
and the signs and houses in which each of these are found.
Look at whether any other planets are also involved with either
of the planets that you are interpreting. This will give you a
broader, more holistic perspective on the influences in your
chart and will enable you to clarify any apparent conflicts in
interpretation.

Sun aspects

Aspects to the Sun reveal an extra dimension in your self-
expression and show how you use your creative impulses.
These aspects can indicate confidence, energy and health issues.
Your potential, willpower, sense of self and your ability to
express your inner power are described through Sun aspects.
Also included is your ability to work with and develop
your potential.

CONJUNCTIONS TO THE SUN

These reveal the ways through which you express your willpower, creative impulses and confidence in a dynamic manner. The signs and houses involved will indicate your approach within the areas of life concerned.

SEXTILES TO THE SUN

The natural state of harmony that occurs between the planets involved allows you to express yourself in a positive and creative manner. This can increase your ability to determine and fulfil your potential through the characteristics of the connected planets and the signs and houses that are involved.

SQUARES TO THE SUN

These reveal challenges to your willpower and difficulties in expressing your potential. However, although these can create blockages to self-expression, if you strive to overcome the issues involved this can bring added strength and determination.

TRINES TO THE SUN

These indicate expansiveness in the areas ruled by the planets concerned, and easy, harmonious self-expression. Known as 'good luck' aspects, Sun trines often reveal a happy-go-lucky emotional nature and positive, mutually beneficial relationships as well as creative talents.

OPPOSITIONS TO THE SUN

These can indicate conflict between the areas of yourself that are involved in the aspect, and clashes of will with other people whom you feel threaten your sense of self. Sun oppositions can point out areas where you feel a need to make yourself heard or noticed through being overbearing or dominant.

> Look at any aspects to the Sun in your birth chart. Which planets, signs and houses are involved? What does this tell you about how you can develop your potential?

Insight

Aspects to the Sun reveal extra information about how you use your self-expression, willpower and creative energy. These also tell you about your energy levels, state of health, and your level of poise and confidence.

Moon aspects

Aspects to the Moon show you the areas in which you feel most intensely. These can reveal information about how you relate to your parents, especially your mother, how you respond as a parent yourself and how you express your nurturing abilities and domestic impulses. Habits, deep-rooted memories and emotional patterns stemming from past conditioning, and your dreams and intuitive gifts will also be revealed through Moon aspects.

CONJUNCTIONS TO THE MOON

These are experienced as powerful emotions, which are expressed through the characteristics, signs and houses of the planets involved. Domestic and family issues, hereditary conditioning, food and eating patterns, and emotional sensitivity are revealed here. Moon conjunctions can pinpoint areas in which you act unconsciously and follow your instincts.

SEXTILES TO THE MOON

These indicate areas in which you are able to express your emotions easily and constructively. Moon sextiles can show close relationships with family and with women, and positive, nurturing friendships.

SQUARES TO THE MOON

Moon squares can reveal the areas in which you feel blocked or held back emotionally. Difficult family relationships, conflicts with women and a too-strong attachment to the past can create either emotional coolness or clinginess, depending upon the other planets, and the signs and houses involved.

TRINES TO THE MOON

These reveal areas of benefit through a harmonious attitude, open emotions, and sociability. Moon trines tend to indicate a harmonious family atmosphere, which gives a sense of inner security and adds to ease in forming friendships. Compassion, emotional sensitivity, a strong intuition and an active imagination are characteristic of Moon trines.

OPPOSITIONS TO THE MOON

These can indicate challenges in relationships with others through feeling unloved or uncared for in the early years. There can be a tendency to project your own negative feelings onto those around you or to dislike qualities in others that you are reluctant to admit having yourself.

> Look at any aspects to the Moon in your birth chart. Which planets, signs and houses are involved? What does this tell you about how you relate to your emotions?

Insight
Aspects to the Moon give information about your feelings and how you express these, your level of intuition, your relationships with family, especially women and the mother-figure, and your abilities to nurture yourself and those around you.

Mercury aspects

Aspects to Mercury reveal the ways in which you think and communicate. Your curiosity, interests and educational aspirations can be found here. Also highlighted are your powers of reasoning and perception, and your memory faculty.

CONJUNCTIONS TO MERCURY

These give strength to your thinking and manner of communication. Mercury orbits close to the Sun and if it is conjunct this can indicate intellectual brilliance. However, if there is less than 4 degrees between Mercury and the Sun this is called 'combustion' and there can be a state of confused thinking due to mental burnout. An exact conjunction is called 'casimi' and reveals profound intellectual abilities. With the other planets, a Mercury conjunction can reveal a powerful interest or abilities in communication in the area of the chart in which these planets are situated and through the lens of the other planet involved in the conjunction.

SEXTILES TO MERCURY

These reveal good powers of reasoning, deduction and communication, which relate to the planets involved and the signs and houses in which these are found. There are likely to be abilities or talents in writing and communicating, and a curiosity that opens up new avenues in friendships and study.

SQUARES TO MERCURY

These can indicate difficulties in communication or problems relating to speech, writing or learning, and education. Perception and judgement can be clouded if there are Mercury squares and this can create rebelliousness or quarrelsomeness in the areas governed by the planets involved.

TRINES TO MERCURY

Mercury trines indicate clear perception and a powerful intelligence that is harmoniously expressed. Diverse interests and a benevolent, expansive manner of communication can help to open up many opportunities for personal growth in the areas governed by both planets involved.

OPPOSITIONS TO MERCURY

These can reveal areas of conflict with others due to differences of opinion or perspective. There may be an inability to see or understand points of view that do not conform to your personal opinions.

> Look at any aspects to Mercury in your birth chart. Which planets, signs and houses are involved? What does this tell you about your thinking and reasoning processes?

Insight

Your powers of reasoning, thinking and communicating are indicated with aspects to Mercury. Your level of curiosity and the way in which you explore your interests or studies are also revealed through Mercury aspects.

Venus aspects

Aspects to Venus indicate how you relate to others, and how you express your affections. Your sociability, attitudes to relationships and romantic partnerships, attractions to others and qualities of charm and personal attractiveness can be understood through Venus aspects. Also included is any fondness for luxury, beauty and pampering. Artistic gifts and talents can also be found here. In a man's birth chart, Venus aspects can reveal the type of woman to whom he is attracted.

CONJUNCTIONS TO VENUS

These indicate friendliness, which leads to easy, nurturing friendships, attractiveness to the opposite sex, powerfully effective emotional self-expression and a caring approach towards others. Venus conjunctions can also pinpoint artistic or creative talents.

SEXTILES TO VENUS

These reveal sociability and creativity, and point out the areas and characteristics through which you can develop your talents in an enjoyable, constructive manner.

SQUARES TO VENUS

These can indicate difficulties and challenges in personal relationships. Blocked emotions or inappropriate emotional attachments and self-expression can be pointed out through Venus squares depending upon the planets, signs and houses involved.

TRINES TO VENUS

Venus trines reveal great harmony of emotional expression and many friendships, along with a charm and personal attractiveness that makes you very appealing to others. There is an innate sympathy and empathy for those around you. These aspects can indicate creative, artistic or musical gifts.

OPPOSITIONS TO VENUS

These can indicate emotional blockages or over-sensitivity, with a tendency to mirror the feelings of those around you. Relationships can be strained and demanding, but consideration for the needs of others as well as your personal needs can be learned through the signs and houses involved in the aspect.

> Look at any aspects to Venus in your birth chart. Which
> planets, signs and houses are involved? What does this tell
> you about your attitudes to relationships?

Insight
Aspects to Venus give extra information about your ways of
relating to other people, and of expressing love, creativity
and harmony. Your sense of beauty is heightened with Venus
aspects, and also ways in which you are likely to indulge or
pamper yourself and others.

Mars aspects

Aspects to Mars reveal how you express the active, dynamic side
of your nature. Energy and drive, skills in active pursuits such as
sports, and levels of aggression or confrontation can be understood
through the aspects to this planet. Positive aspects indicate that
you use the beneficial qualities of Mars in a constructive manner,
whereas challenging aspects can point out the areas in which you
are overly aggressive, short-tempered or impetuous. In a woman's
birth chart, Mars aspects can reveal the type of man to whom she
is romantically and sexually attracted.

CONJUNCTIONS TO MARS

The dynamic energy of Mars is directed through the
qualities and characteristics of the planet with which it is
conjunct and the signs and houses in which both planets are
situated. Mars conjunctions tend to indicate high energy levels
and a powerful channelling of energies, which can be constructive
or destructive, depending upon the other planet involved.
A desire to act swiftly and gain fast results is characteristic.
There is often a tendency towards sudden sexual and romantic
attractions.

SEXTILES TO MARS

The Martian principle of action is expressed constructively
and harmoniously in sextile aspects. There is a drive
towards achievement through hard work and a willingness
to co-operate with others providing they share your vision.
Physical strength and courage are associated with this aspect.

SQUARES TO MARS

This aspect can indicate a short temper and action that is taken
without forethought. Aggressive tendencies are brought to the
surface through frustration when matters are not progressing as
swiftly as you would prefer. Blocks to your achievement of goals
can be overcome through the cultivation of patience and forward
thinking.

TRINES TO MARS

The most positive qualities of Mars are given free expression
in trine aspects. Strength, courage, dynamic pursuit of goals
and a sense of passion for life and for particular interests are
characteristic. Motivation is strong and attracts co-operation
from those in a position to help you along the path to realizing
your goals.

OPPOSITIONS TO MARS

These indicate a tendency to desire to pit your wits against others
and to use force in order to achieve your aims. The competitive
element of your nature is brought to the fore and needs to be used
in order to spur you on while also learning to consider the needs
of others.

> Look at any aspects to Mars in your birth chart. Which planets,
> signs and houses are involved? What does this tell you about
> your motivation and drive?

Jupiter aspects

Aspects to Jupiter indicate how you undergo the process of
expansion and growth. Your beliefs and interests in philosophical
pursuits, religion, higher education and sharing your knowledge
with others are revealed through these aspects. Depending upon
the planets and houses, travel for the purpose of expanding your
mental as well as physical horizons can be indicated. Challenging
aspects, depending on the other planets involved, can point out
traits such as over-spending, over-indulgence in food or luxuries,
or misplaced self-confidence that neglects to take all factors
into consideration. Positive aspects can indicate an optimistic,
cheerful approach to life and an altruistic attitude towards others,
as well as high intelligence and self-confidence.

CONJUNCTIONS TO JUPITER

These reveal your focus for positive thinking, confidence
and benevolence. The planets, signs and houses involved
give indications of how you actively seek to expand your
horizons. Wealth and wisdom are often characteristic of
Jupiter conjunctions.

SEXTILES TO JUPITER

Abundant friendships and interests, and an air of bonhomie are
indicated with Jupiter sextiles. Expansion and opportunities come
through the realm of communication and can be explored through
the planets, signs and houses involved in this aspect.

SQUARES TO JUPITER

These can reveal the areas in which there are hindrances to growth, expansion and development. You may be tempted to over-extend yourself and to lose rather than gain ground in the pursuit of your goals. Taking time to think matters through and take care of seemingly minor details can help you to overcome the challenges of the square.

TRINES TO JUPITER

With Jupiter as the planet of good fortune, and trines as the aspect of good luck, this aspect brings opportunities to develop your talents and to attain a high degree of success and possibly prosperity. The planets involved and the sign and house positions will reveal how you can make the most of your gifts.

OPPOSITIONS TO JUPITER

A tendency to over-extend yourself or to place too much confidence in your own abilities is the hallmark of this aspect. Your optimism, especially if this proves to be unfounded, may create tension with others and can lead to conflict. The planet in opposition and the signs and houses involved will reveal where you need to step back a little.

> Look at any aspects to Jupiter in your birth chart. Which planets, signs and houses are involved? What does this tell you about your urge towards expansion?

Insight

Aspects to Jupiter show the areas in which your attitudes towards, and potential for, growth, increase and abundance are strongly indicated. As Jupiter rules your belief systems and your desire to share knowledge, the houses and signs involved in the aspects reflect your philosophical and teaching approaches.

Saturn aspects

Aspects to Saturn reveal the areas in your life in which you create structure and form, and solidify your goals and ambitions. The qualities of self-discipline and your ability to set out boundaries that help you to feel secure can be viewed through Saturn aspects. Your determination and perseverance, and long-range planning is also indicated. Challenging aspects can point out tendencies to depression or discouragement. Positive aspects indicate an ability to build on your gifts and talents in order to fulfil your potential. Gifts in logic or mathematics can be seen through Saturn's influence.

CONJUNCTIONS TO SATURN

These bring immense self-discipline and an attitude of responsibility in the areas governed by the planets involved. You take these responsibilities seriously and may feel burdened by them, but you are determined to overcome any limitations that may arise.

SEXTILES TO SATURN

Your good organizational skills bring benefits in the areas that are ruled by both planets. You are willing to work hard to achieve your aims and are able to keep your focus on this.

SQUARES TO SATURN

These challenge you to learn to cultivate a positive attitude as Saturn squares indicate obstacles in the areas ruled by both planets. There is a need to work hard to overcome these and to guard against feelings of discouragement or depression. Once approached in a constructive manner, Saturn squares build character and bring enormous self-discipline, which can aid your path to success.

TRINES TO SATURN

These indicate success through the practical application of creative thinking and a sense of responsibility and integrity. Your organizational skills are put to good use in the areas governed by both planets and you are likely to be viewed as a mentor in these fields. The ability to bring plans and ideas into concrete form and structure is characteristic.

OPPOSITIONS TO SATURN

These can indicate conflicts with others through your reserve or stand-offishness in the areas governed by both planets. Saturn oppositions can reveal emotional coldness, which creates misunderstandings and detachment within important relationships. Your challenge is to learn to be more open and trusting.

> Look at any aspects to Saturn in your birth chart. Which planets, signs and houses are involved? What does this tell you about how you deal with practical issues?

Insight

The areas in which you create and overcome boundaries, exercise self-discipline, and cultivate your goals and ambitions are revealed through aspects to Saturn. Issues where you have to deal with blockages, restrictions, or feelings of limitation or constriction are also a focus for these aspects.

Uranus aspects

Aspects to Uranus reveal the areas in which you express your independence and originality. The planets, signs and houses involved determine how and where you exhibit flashes of inspiration, insight and creative thinking. Uranus aspects can indicate scientific or metaphysical gifts and talents, or an attitude of rebelliousness, impetuousness and eccentricity. The areas governed by Uranus aspects are likely to be subject to sudden changes and turnarounds, often dramatic in nature.

CONJUNCTIONS TO URANUS

These indicate flashes of inspiration, strong and innovative mental connections, and gifts in the areas governed by both planets. An attitude of independence, free-thinking and free-spiritedness is predominant. There are likely to be scientific or technical abilities or an attraction to systems such as astrology.

SEXTILES TO URANUS

These indicate ease of self-expression in the areas governed by both planets involved. Opportunities arise through your unusual approach and humanitarian attitude and these allow you to use your creative impulses constructively.

SQUARES TO URANUS

Uranus squares indicate a rebellious, devil-may-care attitude that can create obstacles to your progress. Your challenge is to accept that others also have a valid point of view and to refrain from being dogmatic about the areas in which both planets are situated.

TRINES TO URANUS

These can reveal specific gifts and talents, and flashes of genius in the areas governed by the planets involved. You are able to set out your ideas and goals in a manner that inspires others to support you.

OPPOSITIONS TO URANUS

These can reveal a determination for freedom at all costs, which can have a detrimental effect on relationships through an avoidance of commitment. Clashes with those in authority or an urge to disrupt the status quo can hinder opportunities for progress.

Look at any aspects to Uranus in your birth chart. Which planets, signs and houses are involved? What does this tell you about your attitude towards independence?

Insight

Aspects to Uranus indicate the areas in which you express yourself in unusual and original ways. Your sense of individuality, attitudes of rebellion against limitations, and your idiosyncrasies or eccentricities come to light here, as well as lightning-bolt flashes of insight, innovative thinking, and inner knowing.

Neptune aspects

Aspects to Neptune reveal the areas in your life and the modes of expression through which you follow a desire for transcendence. Artistic, musical and creative gifts and abilities, mystical and spiritual tendencies, intuitive impulses and deep compassion are the hallmarks of positive Neptune aspects. The planet of subtle imagery, Neptune, also rules all elements of the visual arts, so can indicate talents in photography or film-making. Challenging aspects reveal the areas through which you seek to escape from the 'real world' or in which you are prone to deception or illusion, either through yourself or through other people.

CONJUNCTIONS TO NEPTUNE

These can be viewed positively or negatively depending upon the planets, signs and houses involved, but their influence is powerful. Neptune conjunctions can indicate special gifts and talents in the arts, a vivid imagination that is given free rein and a mystical approach to the areas of life that are involved. When used wisely, this aspect brings great depth of insight and compassion. When linked to other challenging aspects, there may be self-deception or a tendency to live in a fantasy world.

SEXTILES TO NEPTUNE

Neptune sextiles indicate a vivid imagination and gifts in areas such as art, writing, photography, music and film-making, which can be developed and can lead to opportunities for personal growth and recognition from others. The other planets, signs and houses involved will reveal how these talents manifest and can be developed. An understanding of others and a sympathetic and empathetic approach is characteristic.

SQUARES TO NEPTUNE

These can indicate escapism or confusion, with difficulties in thinking and seeing clearly, and tendencies towards self-deception. Any reliance on chemical substitutes for relaxation, insight or well-being should be avoided with Neptune squares. The planets, signs and houses involved will reveal the challenges that need to be overcome through self-discipline and determination.

TRINES TO NEPTUNE

Neptune trines indicate a high degree of sensitivity, insight and compassion towards others. There may be a desire to help others less fortunate than yourself in the areas governed by the planets involved. Artistic, creative and musical talents are prevalent with Neptune trines and can open doors of opportunity that bring recognition and success.

OPPOSITIONS TO NEPTUNE

There is likely to be a tendency to project your own issues or problems onto other people, due to an unwillingness to take responsibility for what you have created in your life, or escapist qualities. Relationship difficulties can arise through mistrust, deception on either side or a too-close identification with the partner that hinders the relationship. The other planets, signs and houses involved will pinpoint how this is expressed.

> Look at any aspects to Neptune in your birth chart. Which planets, signs and houses are involved? What does this tell you about your deep-rooted emotional life?

Insight

Neptune aspects highlight the areas in which you experience and express compassion, intuition and the desire for transcendence and inspiration. These reveal how you use your sense of imagery, and also show tendencies to escapism or towards the mystical side of life.

Pluto aspects

Aspects to Pluto reveal how you use your willpower in order to regenerate yourself and your life. The manifestations of the unconscious mind can be seen at work through these aspects, along with your ability to start afresh and remake areas of your life during times of stress and trouble. Any tendencies towards control or manipulation are revealed in the challenging aspects. Pluto has several sides. There is an affinity with: the phoenix, the mythical bird that rises from the ashes of its own destruction and recreates life anew; the scorpion, which destroys mercilessly and at will; and the eagle, which soars above the landscape and sees all in perspective. The aspects reveal which of these motifs are at work in your birth chart.

CONJUNCTIONS TO PLUTO

These are powerful aspects and reveal how you seek to transform yourself and your life. Your willpower and focus are highly developed in the areas governed by the conjunction and there can be extraordinary depth of perception and insight. There may be an affinity for the metaphysical sciences or for psychology, depending upon the planets, signs and houses involved.

SEXTILES TO PLUTO

Talents in all areas of communication are revealed through these aspects and are highlighted by the other planets, signs and houses involved. There is an interest in the ideas and motivations of others, which is used to further understand yourself and the world around you.

SQUARES TO PLUTO

Your tendency to desire to enforce your will on others creates obstacles to your happiness and the achievement of your goals. There may be a do-or-die attitude and a desire to court danger in order to test your inner resources. The planets, signs and houses involved will pinpoint how these aspects are played out. Your challenge is to learn to loosen the reins and relinquish the need to always be in control.

TRINES TO PLUTO

These bring powerful transformational impulses, which are used for making the world a better place for others as well as for yourself. Your desire to connect with others at a profound level may manifest as leadership qualities, healing abilities or intense focus on helping those around you to realize their potential. The other planets, signs and houses involved reveal the areas in which this aspect is most strongly experienced.

OPPOSITIONS TO PLUTO

These can indicate a desire to change those around you, which can be damaging to relationships. Your fear of losing what you have can manifest as a desire for control which can be subtly manipulative and which is met by suspicion or resentment from those whom you wish to be close to. The other planets, signs and houses reveal the areas in which this is manifested. Your challenge is to accept others as they are.

Look at any aspects to Pluto in your birth chart. Which planets, signs and houses are involved? What does this tell you about your capacity for regeneration?

Insight

Aspects to Pluto show the areas in your life in which you experience transformation. Your regenerative abilities, willpower and your management of inner and outer resources are emphasized, as are your abilities to start afresh in each new phase of your life.

Chiron aspects

Aspects to Chiron reveal the areas in which you need to face up to, and deal with, a need for healing. Working constructively with these – rather than negating or ignoring them – contributes to a strong sense of self, an acceptance of who you are and compassion and understanding towards other people. These aspects can lead you to encourage others to overcome their own personal challenges in life and to generate a sense of self-empowerment and self-determination. The inner wound that is represented by Chiron can be used as a springboard to growth.

CONJUNCTIONS TO CHIRON

These indicate a powerful impetus towards healing and self-understanding, which is set in motion through willpower and a confidence in your ability to succeed. Chiron conjunctions, depending on the planets, signs and houses involved, reveal the areas through which you can access your path to healing and wisdom.

SEXTILES TO CHIRON

These indicate the areas in which you can use your desire to help others and can make use of opportunities that enable inner healing and broaden your horizons. The other planets, signs and houses in the sextile will determine how this manifests and is expressed.

SQUARES TO CHIRON

Obstacles and challenges which block your path to healing and self-knowledge are indicated through Chiron squares. Although these may at first glance seem insurmountable, facing these challenges brings about inner strength and self-empowerment. The planets, signs and houses involved reveal how this is experienced.

TRINES TO CHIRON

Facing the element within yourself that needs to be healed becomes the springboard for profound insights and revelations about the nature of your resilience and the growth process that is undergone through these insights. This brings a desire to pass on your understanding to others and ultimately leads to a harmonizing of the diverse facets within yourself.

OPPOSITIONS TO CHIRON

These aspects offer you no choice but to acknowledge and deal with the reasons for your inner wound. Often this is likely to have been inflicted through another person in a betrayal of trust or an act of force or manipulation. Understanding that you can let go of the past and embrace the future is empowering and enabling. The other planets, signs and houses reveal the forum through which this is experienced.

> Look at any aspects to Chiron in your birth chart. Which planets, signs and houses are involved? What does this tell you about your path to wholeness?

North and South node aspects

Aspects to the North node reveal how you relate to social and cultural trends, and how you decipher your place within your social and cultural group. Aspects to the South node reveal how you deal with the repercussions in the present of your experiences or actions from the past. The planets, signs and houses involved will give information about the arenas in which these are experienced.

Look at Jen's aspect grid (Figure 1.6 on page 18). You will see that Jen's Sun (willpower, self-expression, confidence, enthusiasm) is conjunct Mars (action, energy, drive, passion), Mercury (communication) and the Moon (emotions, sensitivity, nurturing). As shown in Jen's chart (Figure 1.5 on page 17). These are all situated in Leo (creativity, drama, extroversion, sociability) in the third house (communication, education, close relationships). This tells us that Jen directs a great deal of energy into communication regarding subjects that she feels passionate about and that she has a deep-rooted desire to nurture the interests and talents of others. The Sun in aspect to Mars and the Moon reveals that she feels a strong sense of life-purpose, is sensitive to the needs of others and aware of her own emotional needs, and that she has a great deal of determination and motivation.

Other planets are also linked to Jen's Sun. Saturn in the twelfth house (discipline, boundaries, imagination) and Uranus in the fifth house (charisma, innovation, creativity) are sextile her Sun, and Chiron in the eleventh house (healing and wisdom, group activities) is in a trine aspect to the Sun. The combination of all these planets indicates a strong sense of self combined with a disciplined approach, a positive, unusual attitude to life and a determination to use her experience in order to help guide others.

Look at your birth chart. Are there any planets that are linked through more than one aspect? What does this tell you about yourself?

10 THINGS TO REMEMBER

1 *An aspect is a significant mathematical relationship between two or more components of your birth chart.*

2 *A conjunction indicates powerful interaction between the components involved.*

3 *A sextile indicates ease of self-expression.*

4 *A square reveals tension or challenges.*

5 *A trine indicates harmony and flow.*

6 *An opposition can indicate conflict, tension or the attraction of opposites.*

7 *Aspects to the Sun emphasize your will and self-expression.*

8 *Aspects to Venus reveal how you relate to other people.*

9 *Aspects to Saturn show how you cope with structure and self-discipline.*

10 *Aspects to Pluto reveal how you respond to major change and transformation.*

Part two
Interpreting a natal chart

6

Self-expression

In this chapter you will learn:
- *about how you express your inner nature*
- *about what motivates you*
- *about how you project yourself outwardly.*

Your instinctive self-expression can be determined through the position of your Sun, your Ascendant and the first house. You express yourself through the forums of each area of your birth chart and of life – from your outward personality through to how you gather and use your resources, how you communicate, act out your creative impulses and your drive for relationships, and the way that you express yourself in your work or career and in the social sphere. However, your primary mode of self-expression, which is interpreted through the factors within this chapter, is used as a springboard for your self-expression in all of the areas of your life.

To be able to discover and be who you truly are is, apart from the instinct to survive, the most powerful drive within us. This leads us to explore the qualities that are most helpful to leading a happy, fulfilled life and to find ways of dealing with any qualities that hinder us from living life to the full. Our self-expression creates bonds with the people around us: in the family, in friendships, romantic relationships and in the workplace. It enables us to recognize and develop our gifts and to use these in order to define ourselves, to find our own personal 'voice' and to use this in ways that are creative and original.

The astrological signs, planets and aspects that help to define your self-expression reveal how you conduct yourself, how you experience and express your spontaneity, self-confidence, creativity and leadership abilities, and indicate how you take steps to motivate yourself.

Your Sun shows how you experience your essential self, how you perceive yourself and the ways through which you follow your path in life and seek to discover and fulfil your potential. Unless your Sun and Ascendant are situated in the same astrological sign, much of this 'inner you' may not be immediately apparent to those around you. The Sun reveals your psychological core, your basic self-expression, your level of confidence, enthusiasm and self-determination, and your avenue towards the growth and development of your personality.

> **Insight**
> The Sun reveals how you perceive and express yourself at the most fundamental level. Your self-expression, the manner in which you experience and direct your will, and your sense of confidence, vitality and enthusiasm are indicated by the position of your Sun.

Keywords for the astrological signs

Aries: you are active and energetic but easily become impatient. You prefer to take the initiative.

Taurus: you are determined and patient, with highly developed senses. You like to plan ahead.

Gemini: you are versatile and fun-loving, interested in everything, and communication is important to you.

Cancer: you are caring but vulnerable, with a strong nurturing instinct. Emotionally you are changeable.

Leo: you are flamboyant, magnanimous and dramatic, benevolent and creative. You like to be the centre of attention.

Virgo: you are practical and discriminating, dedicated to your work, with an ordered, analytical mind.

Libra: you are warm-hearted and sociable, fair-minded and sympathetic, with a desire for harmony.

Scorpio: you are intense and deep-thinking, with an investigative mind. Others find you somewhat mysterious and very determined.

Sagittarius: you are extroverted, independent and friendly, intellectual and philosophical.

Capricorn: you are persistent in reaching your goals and are responsible, hard-working and reserved.

Aquarius: you are a free spirit with an innovative, unusual approach and humanitarian principles.

Pisces: you are a dreamer, compassionate, emotional and with a great deal of sympathy and empathy.

> Look at your Sun sign. Note down some keywords to describe the qualities. What does this immediately tell you about your self-expression?

How others see you: the Ascendant

The Ascendant reveals the characteristics of yourself that you project outwardly. The people around you gain immediate perceptions about your personality, which are reflected through your ascending sign, and only discover the different layers of your personality through the familiarity that comes through spending time getting to know you. We are all multi-faceted beings and the fun and fascination that can be experienced through interpreting a natal chart comes through the insights that can be discovered about the person whose birth chart is being studied and the understanding that each chart can give you an insight into human nature. It is said, however, that we gain a strong impression of someone within the first ten seconds of meeting. This impression is projected through the qualities of the Ascendant.

Look at the astrological sign on the Ascendant. You can use the keywords for the astrological signs for this. How strongly do the qualities that you express of that sign correspond with who you feel you are? What impression do you think other people gain of you on initially meeting you?

Insight

Your Ascendant shows the way in which you express yourself outwardly, and the parts of your personality that people tend to see initially, and assess you by. The personality traits of your Ascendant define the early impressions that others have of you, and show how you project yourself.

Planets in the first house

Sun: self-confident, forceful, headstrong, robust.

Moon: hypersensitive, family-minded, impressionable, emotional.

Mercury: a leader, curious, competitive, enthusiastic.

Venus: charming, attractive, harmonious, loving.

Mars: energetic, strong, wilful, competitive.

Jupiter: lucky, outgoing, enthusiastic, strong-minded.

Saturn: responsible, serious, austere, loyal.

Uranus: unusual looking, individual, striking, magnetic.

Neptune: sensitive, intuitive, mystical, artistic.

Pluto: compelling, mysterious, strong-willed, self-reliant.

Chiron: direct, active, leader, mentor.

Motivation and self-expression

The first house shows your motivation and the ways in which you express your energy and drive, your outward expression and how you focus your personality traits, your outward appearance and your vitality and general state of health. Planets in the first house and aspects to these can offer information about your early life and environment. Planets in conjunction with the Ascendant can also give information about the manner of your birth and your experiences of entering the world, as well as your early childhood.

Aries and Mars are the natural rulers of the first house and looking at the house positions of that sign and planet will reveal how you express yourself through your motivational drives and impulses and how you use your urges towards action. By also taking these factors into consideration, you can gain deep insights into your mode of self-expression and how you seek to fulfil your need to forge ahead.

Insight
Any planets situated in the first house add information about your main focus of self-expression, and can also contribute to your physical looks and build. The Sun in the first house would increase your confidence. Venus in the first house would increase your attractiveness to others.

Look at your first house and note down the triplicity and
quadruplicity, any planets that are situated there and the aspects
which these make to other planets in your birth chart. Are there
any aspects made to your Ascendant?

By studying the Sun, Ascendant and first house, you can discover
a great deal about your self-expression and how others view
you. Understanding the qualities that are revealed through
these lenses of perception can show you how you can develop
these constructively and work with any elements that are
currently limiting you or hindering your sense of freedom of
expression.

Note down brief sentences or keywords that describe your
Sun sign, your Ascendant, and the first house. Consider the
triplicity and quadruplicity in which each of these is situated
as these will explain your temperament and the ways in which
you take action and move forward. Add notes on any planets
in the first house. These will reveal the main influences on
how you express yourself outwardly. Now look at any
aspects that are made to these planets and to the Ascendant.
What does this tell you about how you experience and express
the principles which the planets embody? The combination
of all of these factors reveals how you express yourself
and the impression that other people immediately have
of you.

Insight

Depending on the other planets, signs and houses involved,
aspects to planets in the first house will emphasize or
heighten the qualities and characteristics of your first
house planet. This emphasis creates stress or tension
in challenging aspects, and adds ease of expression in
harmonious aspects.

Increasing harmony

Understanding the factors that motivate you can help you to find avenues for positive change and growth. If the astrological exercise above reveals qualities or modes of expression that you are surprised by or feel uncomfortable with, you can choose to work on those in order to bring out the best in these qualities. Your potential can be developed in any direction you choose and, through pinpointing what is currently effective and what may be causing conflict within you, you can focus on your strengths and determine to strengthen any weaknesses.

Insight

Your strength of motivation, and its focus, is governed by the position of the Ascendant and first house, and your Sun, Mars and Aries in your birth chart. These all show what prompts you to make changes or move forward, and reveal the manner in which you are likely to take action.

JEN'S CHART

Look back at Jen's charts on pages 17–18. Jen's Sun is in Leo in the third house. This indicates that her essential nature is optimistic, sunny-natured and that she thrives on interacting with others and being in the limelight. Positive thinking is her rule of thumb and she tries to see the best in those around her. People gravitate towards her easily because she radiates goodwill and is fun to be with. Highly creative and with a strong sense of drama, she needs to be able to express herself freely and to explore new interests and possibilities. Attracted to bright colours and pretty clothes or objects, she draws attention to her best points and plays down areas of herself that she feels don't show her in her best light. She has a playful side and loves to dress up.

The Sun sign's triplicity is fire. This shows that she is active, dynamic and passionate. The quadruplicity is fixed so she is determined, reliable and can be stubborn in the face of any obstacles that hinder her drive to achieve.

The Sun conjunct Mercury shows an active mind and constructive use of her intelligence. As both of these are in the third house, Jen is an excellent communicator, easily able to connect with those around her, and she is focused on pursuing her creative interests. She is curious and always brimming with plans and new ideas.

The Sun conjunct Mars indicates that Jen has a strong will and is determined to follow her path in life and to achieve her goals. She is dynamic, courageous and tends to leap impulsively into whatever interests her in the moment. Jen allows very little to hold her back and has the motivation to overcome any obstacles in her path.

The Sun sextile Saturn shows that Jen has a great deal of self-discipline, which she uses in order to maintain her focus. She demands a great deal of herself and is willing to push through any limitations in order to move forward towards her goals. She is ambitious to succeed and her positive approach gains her the help and co-operation of those who are in a position to offer opportunities for advancement.

A Sun–Uranus sextile reveals that Jen is an original thinker with a style that is unique to her. Other people view Jen as an exceptional, creative person who is not afraid to take risks. She is independent and finds it hard to be tied down or constricted.

The Sun trine Chiron shows that Jen has an understanding of the area through which she needs to seek healing. Her determination to work with this, and her confidence that this is an element of her growth process, aids her process of self-empowerment. A Sun–Chiron trine also indicates a desire to use her insights in order to help others to heal their inner hurts or wounds.

Jen's Ascendant and first house is Cancer. Jen's outward self-expression is explored through her desire to nurture those around her. She comes across as sensitive, in tune with her emotions and as being easily hurt. Her air of vulnerability coupled with her sunny-natured Leo Sun sign makes others feel protective of her. She finds some inner conflict between her extrovert Leo nature, which adores attention, and her retiring Cancerian Ascendant. Jen likes to be in the thick of wherever there is fun and excitement, but she needs time alone in order to recharge her physical and emotional batteries. She dislikes direct confrontation and tries to be kind to others and to give the benefit of the doubt. Jen's vivid imagination needs expression through her creative impulses otherwise it will manifest as powerful recurring dreams, which prod her into taking notice. The physical appearance that is related to a Cancer Ascendant has two types. The first type which Jen corresponds with is feminine and womanly with rounded curves and a full face – the Moon aspect of Cancer. The second type is slender and willowy, with a long slim face – the Crab element of Cancer.

The ruling planet of Cancer is the Moon. Jen's Moon is in Leo in the third house, which reveals that she communicates her feelings clearly and that her thought processes are coloured by her emotions. She is likely to have a good memory and is aware of any habit patterns that she has unconsciously set up. Jen's Moon sextile Venus, conjunct Mars and trine Jupiter shows that she has powerful emotions, which she tries to express in a harmonious manner, but if she is deeply upset or hurt she may express this through emotional outbursts. She is kind and sympathetic, and has a strong desire to nurture and help others. The Moon square Neptune indicates that Jen's caring nature may make her vulnerable to deception or disillusionment. The Moon opposition MC means that Jen is strongly attached to her home and roots, and finds change difficult to deal with. She needs to feel that she has a secure foundation.

Jen has no planets in the first house in her birth chart.

Venus is conjunct the Ascendant, in Cancer in the twelfth house. This reveals an affectionate, easy-going nature, which easily attracts others. If Venus had been in the first house this would imply a preoccupation with romance as well as creativity and artistic impulses. As Venus is in the twelfth house, the romantic element is slightly suppressed, particularly as Venus is square to Pluto in Jen's fourth house, which reveals that she has a fear of being controlled or manipulated. Jen is likely to need to gain trust in a potential partner before committing herself emotionally. However, her friendliness and good humour attract attention from the opposite sex and she is likely to have many admirers.

Keywords for Jen's self-expression: sunny, optimistic, creative, original (even a little eccentric), fun-loving but with a need to sometimes be alone, self-disciplined, strong-willed, determined, dramatic, caring, emotional, nurturing, reliable, vulnerable.

Look again at the notes you have made about your self-expression. The combination of the factors concerning your Sun sign, Ascendant, first house and aspects, as well as the triplicities and quadruplicities, reveal a great deal about your internal and external nature. Your personality is multi-faceted and you can view each facet as clothes that you put on. Try out the different clothes in this area of your birth chart and consider which ones correspond most closely with what you feel suits you and what you enjoy wearing most. If any restrict you then look for ways in which you can expand the qualities that they bring to the fore. Make a list of the qualities in your self-expression that you enjoy most. Consider how you can harmonize the qualities that you would prefer to be more constructive.

Does your perception of how others view you correspond with how you view yourself?

SELF-EXPRESSION SUMMARY:

▶ *the Sun sign*
▶ *triplicities and quadruplicities*
▶ *the Ascendant*
▶ *planets in the first house*
▶ *ruling planet of the Ascendant, and its aspects*
▶ *aspects from first-house planets and the Ascendant to other planets and the quadrants.*

10 THINGS TO REMEMBER

1 Your initial area for self-expression is your astrological Sun sign.

2 Your Ascendant and first house show your motivation, energy and drive.

3 The way others perceive you is revealed by the first house.

4 Planets in the first house reveal how you express yourself outwardly.

5 The triplicity of your Ascendant indicates how you express your personality.

6 The quadruplicity of your Ascendant shows your approach to life.

7 The ruling planet of your Ascendant gives extra information on your self-expression.

8 Aspects to the Ascendant show the type of energy that you primarily exude.

9 Aspects to planets in the first house reveal whether you find it easy or challenging to express yourself.

10 Aspects to the first house also show how other people see and respond to you.

7

Possessions and earning power

In this chapter you will learn:
* *about your attitudes towards money and possessions*
* *about your inner resources*
* *about how you can boost your earning power.*

Your approach to possessions and earning power, how you recognize and use your inner and outer resources, and your attachment to material belongings are all closely linked to your need for a sense of security and stability. Information about this part of your life can be found in the second house of your birth chart. The astrological sign on the second house, any planets that are situated here and aspects from those planets to other planets, angles and asteroids will tell you a great deal. The ruling planet of the second house sign can give information about the way in which you express and find ways in which to meet your needs. Also included in the second house information are any tendencies towards seeking luxury and comfort, your affinity for beauty in all its forms and your ability to be grounded and to develop staying power.

The natural ruler of the second house is Taurus, with Venus as its natural ruling planet. By looking at the house in which Taurus is situated in your birth chart, you can gather more information about the area of your life through which you seek to accumulate possessions that give you a sense of meaning and comfort, and where and how you utilize the resources at your disposal in order to boost your earning capacity. Venus reveals the areas in which you seek to create a sense of harmony and luxury, and where you choose to follow your heart, and also reveals how you are likely to desire to spend your earnings.

The signs on the second house

Aries: you enjoy new horizons, and are a financial entrepreneur. You are impulsive, and an initiator.

Taurus: you are adaptable, with good business ideas and a practical nature. You can be indulgent.

Gemini: you are full of original ideas for making money and your approach is versatile. You need several interests to keep your attention.

Cancer: you are nurturing towards others and tend to be acquisitive. You are frugal and good with finances.

Leo: you are authoritarian and see your possessions as a power-base. Generosity is a strong attribute.

Virgo: you are cautious and careful with your resources. Co-operative and joint endeavours appeal to you.

Libra: you enjoy creative, cultured business partnerships and work well within these. Money comes easily but may also go easily.

Scorpio: you are resourceful and determined with a talent for making good investments.

Sagittarius: you are considered fortunate with your resources and lucky financially. You are expansive and enjoy co-operating.

Capricorn: you are responsible and careful with your resources, and seek long-term investments. You are ambitious and hard-working.

Aquarius: you find unusual, innovative and original methods of acquiring and using resources. You are technologically-minded.

Pisces: you tend to be impractical and unworldly but are generous, caring and keen on sharing resources.

Your framework

Whether you prefer life to be stable and rooted or whether you enjoy change and variety, there is a need for a framework on which you can build the cornerstones of your life. The second house shows you what you use as your springboard. Self-esteem is developed through experiencing a sense of sureness and confidence, and this emerges through your feelings of rootedness and your ability to express yourself in a way that is natural to you. Security is a quality that comes from within and is closely bound up with your survival instinct and your feelings about being able to be self-sufficient. Outer appearances may give a message to other people, but unless you are able to connect with inner stability, the outer manifestations do not bring lasting feelings of satisfaction and are only experienced as superficial. The resources that are revealed through the second house are not just material and physical. They include your inner, sometimes hidden, resources – particular qualities, gifts or talents, which can help you to move forward in the direction in which you wish to guide your life.

Planets in the second house

Sun: tenacious, determined, resourceful, goal-oriented.

Moon: business-oriented, artistic, home-loving, thrifty.

Mercury: careful, resourceful, practical, motivated.

Venus: extravagant, sensual, loving, upwardly mobile.

Mars: persistent, determined, ambitious, possessive.

Jupiter: resourceful, fortunate financially, generous, extravagant.

Saturn: patient, persistent, prudent, resourceful.

Uranus: risk-taker, unusual resources, group investments.

Neptune: generous, altruistic, idealistic, trusting.

Pluto: accumulative, willpower, determination, financial transformations.

Chiron: patient, practical, helpful, resourceful.

Insight

Planets in the second house reveal how you use your resources and develop your abilities that can be used in the accumulation of money and possessions. These also show your attitudes towards security and stability. A fondness for creating beauty in your environment is reflected through second-house planets.

Look at the astrological sign that is situated on the second house. What does this tell you about your need for security and stability? Consider the triplicity and quadruplicity. Now look at any planets in the second house and their aspects to other planets, asteroids and any angles. Which resources do these signify? Find the house over which Taurus is situated. This will tell you how you use your resources. Note these down.

Working with your earning power

The information you have gathered can be used for the purpose of strengthening your resources and improving your earning power. Firstly, look at the strong, positive points. Think about how you currently use these and how you can further anchor and develop them. If staying power, found through the earth triplicity and fixed quadruplicity, is one of your astrological attributes, think about your goals and how you wish to achieve these. If flexibility, found through the water triplicity and mutable quadruplicity, is among your attributes, consider how you can use this quality in order to increase your earning power. Do you save money in order to feel that you have a secure nest egg? Or are you tempted to indulge in luxuries that make you feel pampered? Examining your birth chart can help you to understand what the term 'security' means to you.

Insight

Look at the sign on the second house, its ruling planet, any planets within the second house, and aspects made to these. Take into account the triplicity and quadruplicity of your second-house sign. For extra information you can look at the position of Taurus in your chart.

Security

If an earth sign is on your second house, you are likely to seek security through possessions, through buying a property, or through working at a job or career that you view as long-term.

If a fire sign is on your second house, you are likely to value adventure more than stability and tend to operate on a 'need to know' basis where your finances are concerned.

If an air sign is on your second house, you tap into your intellectual resources and view networking and information as your source of security.

If a water sign is on your second house, you may find it difficult to settle down in one place for long and view emotional connections with others as your security.

Insight

The triplicity of your second-house sign indicates what motivates you in how you express your sense of security.
An earth sign indicates that this comes through possessions.
An air sign indicates that information networks provide your sense of security.

Using your resources

Once you can see which factors enhance your sense of security, you can understand the qualities that contribute to a sense of well-being. Look at how you can use the factors in your birth chart as resources that can be developed. Aim to develop your attributes, talents and gifts. If there are any challenging aspects to the second house, note these down and consider how you can work constructively with them. What messages do these challenges have for you? How can you turn weaknesses into strengths?

The sensual world

The second house reveals how you express your sensual nature. The five senses are governed by this house, Taurus and Venus. Look at your chart and consider which of the senses is most important to you and whether you are closely attuned to these. Our senses make us feel fully alive. They are a source of communication and can lead into a wholehearted appreciation of nourishment in all its forms – through eating and drinking, through breathing in an uplifting fragrance, through the art of touch, which brings comfort and an awareness of caring and being cared for, through the inspirational effects of beauty and through the ability to listen and truly hear the emotional resonance of voices and music.

> Choose the sense that corresponds most closely with your second-house position. Indulge that sense for a moment. Now consider whether any of your five senses are neglected. Make a resolution to give all of your senses some extra attention.

Insight

The second house governs your senses, so you can discover a great deal about your sensual nature through exploring the sign on, and planets in, the second house. You can also look at the positions of Taurus and Venus in your chart, and the houses that these are placed in.

JEN'S CHART

Look back at Jen's chart on page 17. Jen's second house begins with Cancer. This indicates that she has a strong need for security and views her home as her castle. She has plenty of staying power and is very determined to reach her goals, even though she may tend to move sideways in order to develop extra skills that will come in useful for both her earning power and what she views as her long-term career. Jen keeps some of her plans close to her chest, as she prefers not to tell people what she is working towards until she has accomplished her goals, in case something goes awry. As Cancer is a cardinal water sign, Jen needs to feel emotionally fulfilled in her chosen work and has the ability to inspire those around her with her dynamism and enthusiasm. She can be rather eccentric and unpredictable at times, and takes a humorous perspective on setbacks, which can serve her well.

Jen is strongly attuned to her senses and follows her intuition. Her caring approach means that she is often a repository for the confidences of others. Of the senses, her most highly developed is likely to be that of taste and she enjoys good food, especially when it is nicely presented and smells appealing.

As Cancer is ruled by the Moon, Jen is emotional and has a deep-rooted need to nurture and be nurtured. It is vital for her to feel a sense of emotional fulfilment through her work and, although money and material possessions are important to her, a high salary is not her primary consideration. Job satisfaction and a feeling that she is doing what she loves most are the vital factors for her. Jen's Moon is in Leo in the third house, so she is aware that one of her most effective resources is communication. Networking and emotional support are very useful to the development of both her career and her sense of security, and her sunny approach brings her many friends and supportive colleagues.

The South node is in Jen's second house. As the South node is indicative of habits and tendencies that you bring to bear from the past, which help you to feel secure, Jen started life in a secure environment and is comfortable about the decisions that she makes regarding finances and her career. She is likely to experience feelings of familiarity around certain situations and people – a kind of recognition or a sense of déjà vu, which, with her already keen Cancerian intuition, can be extremely useful.

Taurus is situated over Jen's eleventh house. Friendships and group activities provide a solid framework that enables her to feel secure and sure of herself, and provide her with the sounding boards and feedback that she values highly. She is very much a 'people person' and others find her interesting, reliable and endearing.

Venus is in Cancer in the twelfth house, conjunct the Ascendant. Jen is sensitive and can be shy at times but is able to overcome her introverted side when she is engaged in situations that can further her goals. She tends to hold back a little until she feels comfortable with new people, but once she feels safe she easily opens up and is warmly affectionate. She can be secretive about plans or financial issues.

Jen uses her resources well. She is good at saving money and is likely to invest it wisely. She likes to feel that something is set aside in case it is needed in an emergency, and it worries if her savings run low, even temporarily. Money is spent on material things that enhance Jen's sense of security. She feels comfortable spending money on her home and immediate environment but needs to remember to treat herself occasionally and to be less concerned about counting pennies.

Jen is very good at managing her finances and resources, and is careful not to squander them. She can improve these through using her sensitivity and intuition, and through opening up to new possibilities and horizons which may not necessarily feel 'safe' and predictable but which could lead to unexpected opportunities.

Keywords for Jen's possessions and earning power: tenacious, frugal, determined, emotional, excellent networking skills, nurturing, reliable, intuitive, motivated by emotional fulfilment.

Look again at the notes that you have made about your possessions, security and earning power. The combination of all of the factors concerning your second house, planets and aspects within it, Taurus, Venus and the triplicities and quadruplicities can tell you a great deal about where and how you feel the need for a strong foundation in your life. By exploring these factors you can discover how to fulfil your need for security or stability and can use this as a framework for improving your future financial situation.

Be aware of your inner resources – your qualities such as staying power or versatility and your particular talents and strong points. Make a list of these and see how you can develop them further.

Is there any factor or quality that can be particularly helpful to you?

POSSESSIONS AND EARNING POWER SUMMARY:

▶ *astrological sign on the second house*
▶ *planets in the second house*
▶ *aspects to these planets*
▶ *ruling planet of the sign on the second house*
▶ *position of Taurus in chart*
▶ *position of Venus in chart.*

10 THINGS TO REMEMBER

1 *The second house describes your approach to possessions and resources.*

2 *The resources of the second house can be material, emotional or spiritual.*

3 *As the second-house rulers are Taurus and Venus, looking at their placements can add to your second-house information.*

4 *The sign on the second house reveals your business ability and approach to possessions and resources.*

5 *Planets in the second house reveal how you develop your sense of security.*

6 *The triplicity of the second house reveals how you express your desires.*

7 *The quadruplicity of the second house shows how you work towards fulfilling your desires.*

8 *Aspects to second-house planets show your attitudes towards the material side of life.*

9 *The second house also reveals how you experience a need for security or stability.*

10 *The second house, and position of Taurus and Venus, reveal your sensual nature.*

8

Communication

In this chapter you will learn:
- *about how you think and communicate*
- *about your basic education and your learning path*
- *about how you can communicate more effectively.*

Communication is the method by which we relate to, understand and forge connections with the world around us. This can be verbal, through the spoken and written word, non-verbal, through body language, the senses, the emotions and intuition, or symbolic (in which we associate a symbol with a particular meaning). Communication enables us to gather and share information, express our feelings, give and receive feedback, and to maintain a sense of being recognized and acknowledged. The need to communicate – to hear and be heard – is a fundamental drive.

How you express yourself, your fluency of thought, speech and communication, your basic education and relationships with those close to you, such as siblings and neighbours, are all shown in the third house of your birth chart. This also gives information about how much you rely on technological devices such as the phone and internet, and reveals any likelihood of short journeys that are connected with your urge to communicate. Your approach to learning, and any talents or challenges relating to this, is included in the third house. Consider the astrological sign on the third house and its triplicity and quadruplicity, which reveal your mode of thought and action.

The signs on the third house

Aries: you express your ideas forcefully and can be argumentative and determined. You enjoy the stimulation of heated debates.

Taurus: you are good at creative thinking and express yourself creatively and artistically. You have fixed opinions and can be stubborn.

Gemini: you have an active intelligence and an independent mind. You are versatile and full of new ideas, but these may be scattered so you need to focus.

Cancer: you are communicative in the home environment but need to feel secure before opening up. With your nurturing skills there are close family links.

Leo: you express yourself expansively and creatively, and are dramatic and sociable. You enjoy sharing ideas that will impress others.

Virgo: you have an organized mind, capable of creating order in your thoughts. Your active intelligence enjoys applying itself to details.

Libra: you are highly sociable and friendly, with a sharp creative intellect and sense of justice. You can be extravagant.

Scorpio: you are straight-talking to the point of giving offence, so prefer to remain silent. You are resourceful and persistent, interested in new discoveries.

Sagittarius: you are philosophical and intelligent, with great curiosity. Your ideas are expansive and you share them generously.

Capricorn: you are cautious about what you say and can be introverted. You plan ahead and pursue your ideas with determination.

Aquarius: you have an original, insightful mind and are intuitive, friendly and gregarious.

Pisces: your mind works in subtle ways. Your thoughts are connected with your emotional state. You are intuitive, introverted and mystical.

The astrological sign that rules the third house is Gemini, so look at the houses of your chart in which Gemini and Mercury are found. This gives you information about your main focus for communication and can reveal particular interests and communication skills. As Mercury, named after the messenger god, is the natural ruling planet of the third house, health issues such as dyslexia, speech or hearing problems and nervous disorders can also be seen here. See whether there are any aspects to Mercury as these inform you about your main modes of thinking, speech and writing and can highlight gifts, talents or challenges.

If the third house has no planets within it and there are no aspects to Mercury, this can indicate that you feel shy and cut off from those around you and find communication difficult. The astrological sign on the third house and its triplicity and quadruplicity can help to guide you towards increasing your sense of connection and your communication skills.

Planets in the third house

Sun: communicative, popular, writing abilities, diverse.

Moon: imaginative, eloquent, changeable, sociable.

Mercury: intelligent, quick, multi-faceted, communicative.

Venus: peacemaker, mediator, communicator, networker.

Mars: hasty, restless, independent, opinionated.

Jupiter: intellectual, positive, cheerful, charming.

Saturn: cautious, careful, methodical, meticulous.

Uranus: lateral thinker, unusual, insightful, inspirational.

Neptune: mystical, imaginative, caring, creative.

Pluto: strong-minded, persistent, secretive, insightful.

Chiron: enquiring, communicative, questioning, mentoring.

The planets in your third house show you which qualities are your main sources of interest and also reveal how you express yourself and seek to satisfy your curiosity. Look at any aspects to these planets and at the other houses involved in the aspects. If you imagine that the two houses in aspect are engaged in a dialogue, the nature of the aspect tells you whether this is constructive or whether there is conflict which needs to be resolved through seeking to establish a more balanced perspective.

Insight

Planets situated in your third house show how you choose to pursue what interests you. These also reveal your approach towards learning, and aspects between a third house planet to another planet indicate how easy or challenging that process may be.

Primary modes of communication

The triplicity and quadruplicity of the sign on the third house gives immediate indications of how you communicate.

TRIPLICITIES

Fire (Aries, Leo, Sagittarius): you are quick-thinking, passionate and impulsive in your communication, easily inspired but also easily lose interest. You relish debates and can be quarrelsome, saying things in the heat of the moment.

Earth (Taurus, Virgo, Capricorn): you think before you speak and are careful to ensure that you get your facts right. You are stubborn in your opinions and hold to more traditional ideas. Communication through touch is meaningful for you.

Air (Gemini, Libra, Aquarius): communication is the breath of life for you. You are fascinated by ideas and thrive on discussions. You think fast, aim for co-operation and tend to value logic.

Water (Cancer, Scorpio, Pisces): the emotions are a main source of communication for you and you respond intuitively to the feelings of others. You tend to keep your thoughts and ideas to yourself until you feel sure that these will not be challenged.

QUADRUPLICITIES

Cardinal (Aries, Cancer, Libra, Capricorn): you favour clear, direct communication, and enjoy making decisions. You express yourself confidently and are constructive in your approach.

Fixed (Taurus, Leo, Scorpio, Aquarius): you are willing to try all avenues of expression in order to be understood. Your staying power makes you a strong adversary in debates.

Mutable (Gemini, Virgo, Sagittarius, Pisces): you communicate in a flexible manner and adapt to the person in dialogue with you so that they can relate to what you wish to communicate to them.

Insight

The sign on your third house has a triplicity and quadruplicity that gives you further insight into your primary method of communication. For example Aries, a fire sign, indicates that you think fast, and impulsiveness may lead you to jump to conclusions. Its cardinal quadruplicity gives you skills in decision-making.

Look at the astrological sign, triplicity and quadruplicity on your third house. Now look at any planets in your third house and any aspects which are made to these. What does this tell you about which area and type of communication is most effective for you? Consider how these placements are reflected through your curiosity, thought processes, speech and interests.

Insight

The strengths that you find in your third house, combined with the subjects or issues which most interest you, can be tapped into as a method of deepening your focus and enhancing and developing your skills.

Increasing effective communication

The information that you have explored can be used to improve your communication skills. First, look at the strong points and consider how you can use these more effectively. Are you making the most of opportunities to develop these or are they being overlooked in some way? If, for instance, you are fiery and progressive, think about how you can use this in order to explore new ideas or concepts and connect with like-minded people who can increase your enthusiasm and motivation. If you are earthy and practical, consider how your constructive, straightforward approach can be broadened to encompass particular interests. When you examine your mode of communication it can help you to understand how and why you relate to certain types of people. If you use this information as a method of expanding your horizons, your communication skills will be given more opportunity to develop and become clearer.

> Make a list of your astrological strengths and weaknesses regarding communication. How can you turn the weaknesses into strengths or work constructively with them?

Insight

The sign on the first house, any planets situated within it, and aspects to these, plus Mercury's position in your chart, give you a great deal of information about how you communicate, and what interests you most. You can increase effective communication by developing your strongest points in this area.

JEN'S CHART

Look back at Jen's chart on page 17. Jen's third house begins with Leo. This shows that she expresses herself confidently and positively and derives a great deal of enjoyment through communicating with others. She is a natural optimist who approaches others in an open, friendly manner, and automatically expects the same in return from those with whom she is in dialogue. She has a fun approach and laughs easily, which has the effect of making others warm to her and open up around her. As Leo is a fixed fire sign, Jen holds strong opinions and is an inspired and inspiring speaker, who enjoys sharing her ideas. She responds best to kindness and can be swayed by flattery if it appears to be genuine.

Gemini, the natural ruler of the third house, is situated in Jen's twelfth house. Her urge to communicate is, at times, shifted inwards to explore hidden realms through meditation or through

interests in methods related to the exploration of the mind.
The ruler of Gemini – Mercury – is in Jen's third house.

As Leo is ruled by the Sun, which is situated in Jen's third house, she views communication as a paramount factor in her self-expression, and her manner of communication is strongly bound to her sense of self. She is gregarious and sociable, and is likely to have a wide network of friends. Her sunny nature and optimism mean that she is strongly attuned to positive thinking and tends to expect good things to result from her efforts. Jen's Sun is conjunct Mercury, which means that she is intelligent, with speedy thinking processes, and she is always brimming over with creative ideas and plans. The Sun conjunct Mars in the third house shows that Jen has strong opinions and is eager to forge ahead with any decisions and ideas. Her mode of communication is dynamic and forceful and she gets easily excited and carried away.

The Sun and Mercury in the third house, sextile Saturn in Gemini in the twelfth house, reveals that Jen is in tune with her subconscious and unconscious needs and desires. There is a deep-thinking, introverted side to Jen, which impels her to withdraw at times and think matters through carefully. This aspect, combined with Jen's extrovert tendencies, can be used constructively as it prevents her from rushing into new things too impulsively.

Jen's Sun and Mercury are both sextile Uranus, which is in the fifth house. This reveals that Jen has an innovative, intuitive approach and is eager to make the most of opportunities that come unexpectedly. As the fifth house governs creativity, play, the arts and drama, that Jen's chosen career is in film-making is hardly surprising. Her gifts in communication bring many opportunities for excitement, dissemination of ideas, sharing of skills and creative self-expression.

The Sun and Mercury trine Chiron indicates that Jen has a great deal of insight into the human condition and uses this to help empower those around her. Much communication is likely to involve healing, particularly through complimentary therapies, and Jen is a firm advocate of positive thinking as a fundamental part of the healing process. Chiron in the eleventh house, in Aries, reveals an involvement in individuals or groups that take an innovative approach to self-understanding and self-empowerment.

Jen's Moon is also in the third house. She responds to emotional impetus and is innately kind and caring in her approach. She has a desire to like and be liked and has a talent for networking and for forging connections between those around her who she feels are kindred spirits. The Moon conjunct Mars increases Jen's emotional approach in communication. She can become hurt and upset easily if others do not treat her sensitively, and when this happens she is likely to become angry and then withdraw until she feels positive again.

The Moon sextile Venus shows that Jen is caring and affectionate and is warmly nurturing. Venus in Cancer in the twelfth house, conjunct the Ascendant, reveals a highly sensitive, emotional, vulnerable aspect to Jen's usually expansive personality. She needs time alone in order to recharge herself after a period of extensive communication and activity. Once this has occurred she bounces back with renewed vigour.

Jen's Moon trine Jupiter in Sagittarius in the sixth house reveals that much of her communication and emotional sustenance are focused on and derived through her work. Her positive approach brings many opportunities for expansion and she is well liked and respected by those she works and associates with.

The Moon square Neptune in the sixth house shows that Jen needs to be careful about trusting people who may use her knowledge, contacts and generosity of spirit to meet their own ends. This aspect can indicate incidents of deception, which have an effect on her feelings about her career. Fortunately, the many positive aspects in Jen's chart show that these negative feelings will not overwhelm her innate positivity, but the Moon/Neptune square poses a warning to be on guard against being taken in by illusions.

The Moon and Mars opposition MC in Pisces reveals strong bonds between Jen and her family and these give her the confidence to aim high. She may be nervous about leaving the nest but has a strong foundation to her life. The close communication strengthens Jen's confidence and opens her mind to opposing views and opinions.

Mars is trine Jupiter in the sixth house. Jen communicates forcefully and expansively about her chosen work and is highly motivated to succeed. The Mars/Neptune sixth house square reveals, again, the possibility of deception and this is likely to be met by Jen with an angry and uncompromising response. Mars is also trine Chiron in Aries, eleventh house, which indicates that health issues regarding energy are an issue that she communicates about and is eager to rectify.

Keywords for Jen's communication focus and skills: intelligent, energetic, inspired, optimistic, positive, strong-minded, confident, intuitive, thoughtful, caring, sometimes over-trusting, sensitive, career-oriented, health-conscious, networking, sociable.

Take another look at the notes you have made on your mode of communication and particular areas of focus. The combination of all of the factors of your third house, Gemini, Mercury and the triplicities and quadruplicities can give you a great deal of information about how you think and speak, what your interests are and how you can develop your communication skills effectively. These skills can open doors to you in all areas of your life – with your family, friends, romantic relationships and business associates.

Consider the communication resources that you have and look at how you can work with or strengthen any challenges or weaknesses. List your strongest points and see how you are using these now and how they can be further developed.

What stands out most predominantly in your communication and interests?

COMMUNICATION SUMMARY:

▶ *astrological sign on the third house*
▶ *ruling planet of the sign on the third house*
▶ *position of Gemini in chart*
▶ *position of Mercury in chart*
▶ *planets in the third house*
▶ *aspects to planets in the third house.*

10 THINGS TO REMEMBER

1 *Communication in your chart includes verbal, written or communication through technology.*

2 *The third house reveals your communication strengths and weaknesses.*

3 *Your thinking and deductive qualities are revealed in the third house.*

4 *Third-house communication includes relationships with siblings and neighbours.*

5 *Your attitudes and approach to education are shown through this area of your chart.*

6 *The sign on your third house shows how you think and communicate.*

7 *Planets in the third house reveal how you express yourself through communication.*

8 *Aspects to the third house reveal your communication strengths, weaknesses and gifts.*

9 *You can use your third-house placement to improve your skills.*

10 *The position of Gemini and Mercury in your chart adds depth to your understanding of how you communicate and what interests you.*

9

The home and roots

In this chapter you will learn:
- *about your roots and foundation*
- *about your home and family life*
- *about how your foundations are a springboard to your future.*

Our sense of roots provides the foundation for our future development. The family and home create our first experiences of self-image, which develop and have a profound effect on later relationships. Family life teaches us how to find our place within a group, how to give and receive love and affection and deal with disapproval and discipline, and sets up patterns that are reflected in our feelings about ourselves and our responses to those around us. Families have their own form of structure and hierarchy, and each individual acts as a mirror to the rest.

Cultural mores and methods of upbringing also give us a sense of our roots. Ancestry, history, tradition and the mining of information about the past all contribute to our understanding of who we are and where we come from. This, along with family and later with our peers, forms the basis for a sense of belonging.

The area of your birth chart that can most effectively demonstrate this is the fourth house. The fourth house describes your early life, your roots, family, domestic interests and nurturing tendencies. Special interests in land and property, archaeology and history are also associated with the fourth house because these subjects offer information about the past. The first relationship is usually with the mother and this house can reveal the form that this relationship has taken and how it is reflected in your own approach to nurturing.

Insight

The astrological sign at the beginning of your fourth house shows the foundation that your self-perception and relationships with others are built on. This house gives information about how your family, roots and past have shaped you and helped create patterns that you trace throughout your life.

The signs on the fourth house

Aries: you like to be boss at home and can be combative but stimulating. You like gadgets, especially domestic technology.

Taurus: you are creative and artistic in the home, and beauty is important to you. You have a fondness for luxury and are protective towards the family.

Gemini: you may move home several times as you enjoy the stimulation of new environments. The home may be an intellectual base with much communication.

Cancer: you are caring and devoted to your home and family, and adept at domestic issues. You may be possessive or bossy with your loved ones.

Leo: you use the home as your social and creative base, and are loving and magnanimous. You view yourself as the ruler in the home.

Virgo: you may work from home or use this as a base for work. There is much intellectual activity in the home. You tend to be house-proud.

Libra: your home must be visually appealing and comfortable. You are fair-minded and loving in family life, and insist on equality.

Scorpio: you are powerfully protective of your family and a strict taskmaster. Your home is your sanctuary and you are private about your emotions.

Sagittarius: you are benevolent and use the home as an intellectual base. You are expansive and need freedom to travel.

Capricorn: you are orderly and organized, and like your home to be neat and tidy. You are likely to be strict about home rules.

Aquarius: the home life or environment may be unusual and social activity takes place here. The home may be a base for group activities.

Pisces: you are a private person and view your home as a sanctuary. You may create artistic or unusual surroundings.

> Look at the sign on your fourth house and consider what its qualities and characteristics can tell you about your home and family life.

The natural rulers of the fourth house are Cancer and the Moon, so look at where these are situated in your birth chart. This tells you about your emotional responses, your need for (and facility for) nurturing and a solid foundation, and about your attitude towards past experiences that have helped to shape your personal and world view. Cancer and the Moon are sensitive and relate to deep feelings. The houses where they are found and the sign in which the Moon is situated give information about areas of your life in which you invest a great deal of emotion and through which you seek to nourish yourself and those around you.

The Moon is changeable by nature, so the area of your chart where the Moon is situated is likely to be susceptible to fluctuations in mood. For instance, Cancer in the fifth house indicates that your nurturing abilities are focused in the realms of children, play, drama and teaching, and that you enjoy passing on what you have learned in order to foster the abilities of others. The Moon in Gemini indicates that you think fast and have many interests but that you tend to get bored easily and need frequent new sources of stimulation. Its house position can tell you what the main focus of these interests are. The Moon is also associated with personal or unconscious inherited memories. Consider aspects to the Moon, even if it is not situated in the fourth house.

Planets in your fourth house reveal much about your early physical environment and also your psychological conditioning. Your habit patterns, emotional responses and imprinting can be gauged from fourth-house influences. Your feelings about food, which are closely bound to the nurturing instinct, can also be explored here.

Planets in the fourth house

Sun: nurturing, home-making, sensitive, intuitive.

Moon: homely, domesticated, protective, nurturing.

Mercury: shy, introverted, home-loving, domesticated.

Venus: home-maker, family-oriented, warm, considerate.

Mars: practical, robust, argumentative, crusader.

Jupiter: harmonious, family-minded, trusting, caring, home-loving.

Saturn: responsible, stable, dependable, unself-confident.

Uranus: extended family, stimulating home life, independent, free-living.

Neptune: caring, compassionate, family secrets, love of nature.

Pluto: home as retreat, private, early upheaval, control in home.

Chiron: quiet, introverted, need for security, family issues.

Insight
Any planets in the fourth house give information about your conditioning and instinctive responses, and the environment in which you spent your childhood and early years. They also show natural tendencies towards following habit patterns, and reveal your nurturing abilities.

Primary modes of exploring your roots

Exploring the triplicity and quadruplicity of the sign on your fourth house can help you to understand your attitudes towards home, family, roots and nurturing.

TRIPLICITIES

Fire (Aries, Leo, Sagittarius): there are likely to be debates and arguments in the home, which flare up quickly and are soon forgotten. Inspiration can be gained through a family member.

Earth (Taurus, Virgo, Capricorn): you are most comfortable in a stable environment where everything has its place. Practical issues and material concerns are important.

Air (Gemini, Libra, Aquarius): you need a stimulating environment, and communication and co-operation are vital to you. You use the home as a base for socializing.

Water (Cancer, Leo, Scorpio): you are highly sensitive to the moods of those around you and feel tearful or resentful if your needs are not met. You like to make your environment feel welcoming and to reflect your personality.

QUADRUPLICITIES

Cardinal (Aries, Cancer, Libra, Capricorn): you make your wishes and opinions heard, and are determined to be involved in family matters and decision-making.

Fixed (Taurus, Leo, Scorpio, Aquarius): you tend to want to impose your will in order to have matters go your way. Change is hard for you and you prefer a stable base.

Mutable (Gemini, Virgo, Sagittarius, Pisces): you cope well with changes and are accommodating regarding the needs and wishes of other family members.

Insight

The fourth-house sign, any planets situated there, and aspects to these, informs you about your roots. For instance, Cancer on the fourth house shows a home-loving nature and a deep-seated desire to create an environment of comfort, nurturing and security that has its basis in your early conditioning.

Note down your perceptions of the triplicity and quadruplicity of the astrological sign on the fourth house. Now look at any planets situated in this house and their aspects. Write down a few keywords. What does this tell you about how you relate to and understand your home life, early years, relationship with your mother and your sense of belonging? How does this information affect your current life and views?

Insight

The triplicity and quadruplicity of your fourth-house sign both add insight into your emotional patterns and natural tendencies. Your level of comfort in particular environments, your attitudes towards home and family, and your need for stability and security or change and stimulation are all revealed through these.

The springboard to the future

Your early experiences provided the foundation for future expectations. The exercise that you have just done can reveal how you feel about your roots and early life, and which patterns of thinking and emotional responses have been set in motion in the past. Consider how you have responded to these stimuli. You may be unconsciously repeating patterns which were based on perceptions and conditioning laid down in the past. Or you may be rebelling against these and taking steps to cultivate a very different approach to that which was used by your family. Your attitudes towards home-making, parenting, nurturing and cultivating a sense of belonging can be changed if you feel this is helpful through understanding why you have developed these patterns.

Positive aspects to the fourth house indicate a happy home life, which then reflects in your future attitudes towards, and experiences of, home-making and nurturing. Challenging aspects can indicate that the early years were difficult, which sets up feelings of self-doubt and insecurity, which need to be acknowledged. Looking at the strengths in your birth chart can increase your confidence and help you to find ways in which to empower yourself.

As well as giving information about the beginning of life, the fourth house can also give you a preview of your final years. Whereas your early years are influenced by the conditioning that was imposed on you by your parents, family and culture, the experiences and emotional habit patterns of your later years are strongly influenced by the emotional and mental habit patterns that you yourself have created through long use. Becoming aware that you are perpetually creating a new foundation in each moment can help you to use your astrological strengths in order to make this as constructive as possible.

Insight

Your early years create the emotional patterns which carry through into later life, because these become engrained during childhood. The various facets of the fourth-house

(Contd)

influences reveal these patterns, and understanding this can help you to make changes to your attitudes if these patterns are not constructive or helpful.

List your astrological strengths and weakness with reference to your sense of roots and foundation. Consider how you can develop these in the light of your home and family life. How can you use these to increase an atmosphere of harmony and belonging?

JEN'S CHART

Look back at Jen's chart on page 17. Jen's fourth house begins with Virgo, a mutable earth sign. She likes her home environment to appear ordered and needs to know where everything is. Jen's sense of security and stability is based on a stable home life and co-operative relationships within the family structure. She uses her home as a place of rest and retreat, where she can focus on maintaining her health and enjoying a balanced diet. Jen is comfortable about her part in family decisions and uses her home as the basis for intellectual and work pursuits. However, she tends to prefer not to use the home as a place for social gatherings but views it as her sanctuary where she can relax and get to the nitty-gritty of ironing out details in any plans she is involved in.

Cancer is on Jen's first and second houses, which indicates that her sense of self and her ability to access and use her resources are both strongly bound up with the security that was fostered in her early years. Jen's experiences of being nurtured have led her to wish to also nurture those around her and she is supportive and caring.

As Cancer is ruled by the Moon, which is in Jen's third house, she is open to a great deal of communication and easily expresses her feelings and emotions. Jen's Moon in Leo highlights her dramatic and creative qualities and gives power to her emotions. Jen's chosen room for taking her own space is likely to be a treasure trove of objects or artefacts that she finds beautiful and which hold happy memories for her. The positive aspects to Jen's Moon indicate a harmonious home and family life, and constructive emotional patterns that have been laid down through genuine caring and nurturing from her family. This helps Jen to feel secure and provides a sound foundation for confidence and trust.

Jen's Moon is conjunct Mars, sextile Venus, trine Jupiter, square Neptune and is opposite the MC. As her Moon is in the third house, you can discover in Chapter 8 how this directly affects Jen's communication skills. In the context of Jen's sense of roots, this reveals that she has received a great deal of positive reinforcement and mentoring, and that the confidence and optimism which has been developed as a result has contributed to her mostly gregarious nature. As she learned early on to be trusting, the Neptune square can make her susceptible to predators, but the immensely harmonious aspects, combined with her innate intuition and ability to shrug off disappointments and learn from these, means that she is able to recover. She uses unpleasant experiences as a future deterrent. This enables Jen to retain her sense of security despite upsets or upheavals.

Pluto is in Jen's fourth house, at the very beginning of Libra. Co-operation and partnership are powerful values in her life and she views these as a foundation for her home, creative and working life. Pluto in the fourth house can indicate an upheaval in early life, which leaves Jen with an urge to be in control of her environment. She prefers her home to be a place where she can be quiet, peaceful and private, and, despite her usual outgoing approach, Jen needs to withdraw at times in order to access her inner resources.

The Venus square Pluto heightens Jen's perception, but as Venus is in the twelfth house it is likely that a past emotional trauma, which is kept private, is the overriding reason why Jen sometimes feels a need to withdraw. Her strategy for dealing with this is to be cautious about opening up too quickly in romantic relationships.

Jupiter in the sixth house square Pluto can indicate over-confidence at times, which can lead to Jen running out of resources that she has been taking for granted. She gives a great deal of herself, especially regarding her work, and needs to remember to take care of herself and direct her considerable nurturing capacity into meeting her own needs. Neptune in the sixth house, sextile Pluto, indicates that Jen has tremendous emotional resources and is able to use her visionary abilities with power and aplomb. This aspect is very helpful to Jen's film-making career.

Pluto is trine the North node, which shows that Jen is able to tap into the Zeitgeist and has a powerful sense of timing. Her clarity of vision and understanding of what motivates people enables her to see what is needed at the time and act accordingly. The square between Pluto and the Ascendant challenges Jen to be objective about herself and to refrain from imposing her will on others.

Keywords for Jen's home and roots: nurturing, kind, secure, strong foundation, needs a sanctuary, health-conscious, organized, creative, early trauma, trust, caring, visionary, strong-willed.

Look again at the notes you have already made on your early environment, home, roots and nurturing issues. Exploring your fourth house, Cancer, the Moon and the triplicities and quadruplicities can reveal what has created your foundation in life and how you have used this as a springboard to future growth. Looking at the planets and aspects can show you the qualities that you are working with and pinpoint constructive or unhelpful patterns of thinking or behaving.

Consider all of these resources put together. How can you more effectively use your strengths and add strength to your weaknesses? The foundation you experienced as a child can be worked with in order to help you to empower yourself as an adult, regardless of the experiences you encountered. Look again at your strengths and ask yourself how you used these in the past, and how you are using these now.

THE HOME AND ROOTS SUMMARY:

▶ *astrological sign on the fourth house*
▶ *triplicity and quadruplicity*
▶ *ruling planet of the sign on the fourth house*
▶ *position of Cancer in birth chart*
▶ *position of the Moon in birth chart*
▶ *planets in the fourth house*
▶ *aspects to planets in the fourth house and the IC.*

10 THINGS TO REMEMBER

1 *Your roots and history provide the foundation for your life.*

2 *Your early experiences shape your adult perceptions and attitudes.*

3 *Your sense of belonging and grounding is shown at the Nadir (IC) of your chart.*

4 *The fourth house reveals your roots, upbringing, and nurturing and domestic gifts.*

5 *The sign on your fourth house shows your essential feelings about fourth-house issues.*

6 *Any planets in your fourth house reveal how you express yourself in this area.*

7 *The positions of Cancer and the Moon in your chart indicate your approach to caring and nurturing.*

8 *Aspects to the fourth house heighten the qualities of the components involved.*

9 *The fourth house governs your early conditioning and imprinting.*

10 *The fourth house gives information about your later life, based on the formation of early patterns.*

10

Recreation, romance and creativity

In this chapter you will learn:
* *about your sense of creativity and romance*
* *about your sociability and any latent talents*
* *about how to tap into your fun-loving side.*

Play has an important role in life and its value can easily be forgotten in our society, which places an emphasis on work, output and achievement. Play provides an outlet for relaxation, an effective form of stress-relief and a way in which to reconnect with the sheer joy of being alive.

As children we learned through play. The processes of curiosity and exploration, the art of co-operation, the ability to communicate and the development of skills are all part of the purpose of play. As we grow up, play is often viewed as something extraneous, which has to be somehow fitted into leisure hours or vacation times. Yet we can reconnect with the childlike, fun, playful aspect of ourselves through merely cultivating an attitude of openness and seeing the possibilities for enjoyment in everyday tasks or pursuits.

In your birth chart, the main area through which you can explore recreation, entertainment, creativity and romance is the fifth house. This governs your desire and ability to be light-hearted and creative, and reveals the area of life in which you are most likely to shine and where you wish to do well and be recognized and applauded by others. The fifth house is ruled by Leo and the Sun, which deal with your self-expression, your creativity, sense of drama and your attitude towards romance. Anatomically, Leo rules the heart, the symbolic seat of love and your romantic impulses, and the fifth house indicates where and how you 'put heart' into your self-expression, your life and your interests. Physical children or creative impulses are also governed by the fifth house, which can indicate your attitude towards children and creativity and any predisposition towards teaching. Essentially, the fifth house informs you of what you feel most passionate about.

The signs on the fifth house

Aries: you are active and dynamic, sporty, flirtatious, creative and original, a leader and initiator of ideas and plans that involve others.

Taurus: you are romantic and sensual, and you love deeply. Your practical side needs results for your artistic/creative expression.

Gemini: you are the life of the party, fun-loving, sociable and friendly. Your versatile creative intellect needs creative expression.

Cancer: you are romantic, idealistic and easily hurt, possessive in love and with a penchant for emotional drama.

Leo: you are highly dramatic and romantic, attention-loving and magnanimous. You are highly creative and may be good at sports.

Virgo: you do not give your heart easily and are cautious and discriminating. You are a perfectionist and apply your talent for preciseness creatively.

Libra: you love to be in love and need to feel part of a partnership. You are warm and friendly, fair-minded and refined, with creative/artistic talents.

Scorpio: you are caring, intense and emotional, though you try to keep this hidden. You can be possessive and dramatic.

Sagittarius: you express your creativity through the realm of ideas and are active in pursuing these. You are active and prone to extravagance.

Capricorn: you can be upwardly mobile in your relationships and recreational activities. Beneath your practical, careful surface is a sensual nature.

Aquarius: you are friends with everyone, gregarious and stimulating, full of ideas and creative projects. You collaborate well and have unusual liaisons.

Pisces: you are unselfish and loving, private about your emotional attractions and are an idealist and romantic. Your artistic/creative talents are highly developed.

Insight

The sign on your fifth house cusp indicates the focus for your need for recreation, pleasure, play and creative exploration. It reveals how you express yourself, and shows the area in which you enjoy being in the spotlight. Attitudes towards romance and children are also reflected here.

Look at the astrological sign on your fifth house and think about what the characteristics of this sign can tell you about your sense of play, your creativity and your urge towards romance.

As the natural rulers of the fifth house are Leo and the Sun, look at where these are situated in your birth chart. These can tell you about where and how you feel an urge to 'be yourself' and to express yourself creatively and dramatically. Your Leo position will inform you about the area of life in which you are able to be extrovert, to display yourself to others in the hope of being recognized for who you really are. It reveals your mode of creative and dramatic expression, and whether or not you enjoy being in the limelight. If Leo is on the twelfth house, for instance, you may hide your light under a bushel or prefer that while your achievements are recognized, you can retain your privacy and avoid having a public 'face'. Leo on the fifth house reveals that you are an extrovert, the life and soul of any gathering, and have a powerful need to gather people around you who will strengthen your self-belief and confidence. This position will indicate a strong creative impulse and a highly romantic streak.

The Sun reveals your intrinsic self, your inner nature, and is indicative of your sense of purpose in life. The sign and house in which your Sun is found can tell you how you seek to express yourself with integrity and in which area you are most likely to allow your talents to shine through. Positive thinking, confidence and creativity are all expressed through your Sun position. As the Sun also indicates your path of inner development, the creative impulses that are reflected in your birth chart are linked with your desire to grow as a person and fulfil your potential.

Planets in the fifth house describe how you express your creativity, sense of drama, romantic impulses and attitude towards children. The characteristics of any fifth-house planets indicate the most meaningful channels for focus with your creative gifts, and the avenues through which you are able to express yourself in a playful way.

Planets in the fifth house

Sun: shows that you are creative and confident, with strong self-assurance. You are a romantic and tend to fall in love easily. You like to be the centre of attention.

Moon: shows that you are highly imaginative and have a strong bond with children. You are a romantic but can be changeable. Arts, crafts and cooking are among your creative talents.

Mercury: reveals you are a creative thinker and full of interesting ideas, which you are able to put into practice. You are fun and entertaining, with a tremendous sense of drama. There may be talents in writing and communicating.

Venus: shows you are a die-hard romantic and fall in love very easily. You are easily flattered and are likely to be surrounded by admirers. The Arts, drama or music are ideal channels for your creative energy.

Mars: reveals that you have an active love-life and take the initiative in your romantic and creative pursuits. You put a great deal of energy into your creative and romantic impulses, and are confident and dynamic.

Jupiter: indicates romantic enthusiasm, expansion and good fortune through your creative interests, which can be used profitably. You are excellent at gaining support and may be a benefactor in artistic or dramatic areas. Teaching abilities are likely.

Saturn: shows that you are self-disciplined and structured about honing your creative skills. You take your passions seriously and are likely to gain respect in your creative field. Romantic attraction to an older partner is likely.

Uranus: reveals a tendency to fall in love suddenly, though you find commitment a challenge. You are innovative and inspired where your creative interests are concerned and have a tremendous sense of drama.

Neptune: shows a highly romantic disposition with a strong idealistic streak. There may be talents in the arts and in film-making or acting. You become easily absorbed in your creative interests.

Pluto: indicates a passionate nature with powerful attractions. You are intensely dramatic and can be dominant in relationships. It is likely that you are extremely talented and creative.

Chiron: reveals an interest in the healing qualities of creativity and the arts. It is important for you to make time for leisure and play and you tend to view love as a panacea. You are committed in your romantic and creative self-expression.

The triplicities and quadruplicities of the astrological sign on your fifth house can help you to further understand how you express yourself romantically and creatively, and the areas of recreation, leisure and entertainment which you are most likely to be attracted to and find inspiring. Taking these into account will enable you to gain a great deal of information about how you use the qualities of the fifth house.

Insight

The fifth house is ruled by the Sun, which governs your self-expression, confidence levels, and the development of your individuality. The sign in the fifth house, planets within it, and the position of the Sun in your chart all contribute towards the focus of your creative expression.

Look at the triplicity and quadruplicity of the sign on your fifth house and any planets that are situated here. Note whether these make aspects to other planets. You will now have a strong sense of how you express yourself creatively and romantically.

Insight

The fifth house, and any planets within it, emphasize romance, because the forces of attraction are strengthened here. Who and what attracts you, and how you respond to this, can be found in this house. It reveals what brings about feelings of connection, absorption, pure joy and a sense of discovery.

Having fun

Your exploration of the fifth house so far will have revealed a great deal about your romantic tendencies and needs, and your creative impulses. These are connected to your sense of play. Romance (a separate, though linked, issue to love, which will be explored in Chapter 12) is often viewed as a game in which attraction is felt and possibly expressed in the hope of reciprocation. When the emotions become more seriously involved, the heady spur of initial attraction gives way to the desire for a deeper understanding of the partner. The fifth house element of romance can apply to any form of attraction as it involves a feeling of connection and an urge to commune with the person or object of affection. For this reason, the creative urge is also governed by the fifth house. When we are engaged in a creative interest, time slips by unnoticed and there is a sense of absorption and fascination which is joined with a playful 'What if?' attitude which can lead to immense growth, positivity and confidence.

The influences of your fifth house can reveal what entertains you, what you can engage with in a playful way and gain pleasure from. By exploring these you can discover how to enhance the feelings of pleasure in your life.

Positive planetary aspects to your fifth house indicate a healthy approach to the playful elements of yourself and an ability to tap into your light-hearted side. These show the qualities that can be used creatively in order to enhance your life. Challenging aspects point out the areas in which you may take yourself too seriously and need to 'lighten up' a little, or can indicate difficulties with creative self-expression.

Insight

Your sense of play recaptures the feelings of pleasure, enjoyment and absorption of childhood. Play can be experienced through expressing your creativity, through friendships or a recreational interest that helps you to feel good. Positive aspects to fifth-house planets reveal which areas accentuate your playful, fun-loving nature.

> Make a list of what you consider are your astrological strengths
> and weaknesses regarding romance, recreation and creativity. Now
> think about how you can work constructively with these in order to
> make more use of the potential. See whether any talents are present
> which you could develop. Consider how you can add strength and
> impetus to any gifts or talents which you are already aware of.

JEN'S CHART

Look back at Jen's chart on page 17. Jen's fifth house begins with
Libra, a cardinal air sign. She is communicative about her interests
and creativity, and is drawn to create beauty and harmony and to
explore areas that are meaningful to her. Jen's talent for co-operation
is coupled with enthusiasm and innate friendliness, and other
people easily warm to her and want to please her. Jen finds that
being open and pleasant brings rewards in terms of friendships with
like-minded people and assistance through networking. She dislikes
and avoids confrontation or uncouthness. For Jen, creativity is very
much related to her personal self-expression and she seeks to keep a
balanced viewpoint and to ensure that the doors of communication
are always open. She views her creative side as a main form of
recreation and takes pleasure in exploring new ideas and bringing
these to fruition. If you look at Jen's chart, you will see that her fifth
house and its opposite partner, the eleventh house, occupy more
space than the other houses. This reveals that a vast quantity of her
focus and sense of self is expressed through these two areas.

Leo begins on Jen's second house, which deals with her resources
and ability to generate income. This, coupled with her fifth house,
shows that Jen's creative interests are closely bound with her
earning capacity. This bodes well for her career as a film-maker
because the fifth house includes the dramatic arts.

As Leo is ruled by the Sun, which is in Jen's third house, her intrinsic
nature and self-expression are closely bound with her ability to
use her resources in a creative manner and through all forms of
communication. Jen is confident and positive, and has a strong belief
in her ability to direct the course of her life. Sunny-natured and

optimistic, she tends to attract kindred spirits who can help her to achieve her goals. The Sun in Leo is a dramatic combination and this adds impetus to the creative focus of her fifth house.

Jen's Sun is conjunct Mercury, Mars and the Moon in the third house. A great deal of Jen's energy is put into communication, action and following her intuition. She is good at 'walking her talk' as she needs to feel that there will be practical, tangible results for her efforts. The combination of these planets in Leo brings a strong affinity for the dramatic arts and for creativity in general. Jen clearly has a 'feel' for what will work and follows her ideas through.

Uranus is in Jen's fifth house. Romantically, this indicates that Jen falls in love easily and is likely to experience the Uranian thunderbolt of love at first sight. However, she has an aversion to being tied down as her freedom is vitally important to her. It is possible with this placement that Jen feels her creativity needs a great deal of personal space and freedom in order to be fully expressed and she may have concerns that a relationship could impinge on, or distract from, her creative flow. She is extraordinarily innovative, brimming with unusual ideas and concepts, which she is eager to bring into form. Jen feels passionately about her interests and is easily inspired. She has a strong humanitarian impulse and a genuine desire to help others.

Jen's Uranus is sextile her Sun in the third house, creating a harmonious link between her essential nature and sense of self and her innovative, intuitive communication skills. She has the inspiration and motivation and uses these in creative, practical, tangible ways.

Uranus is also sextile Jen's Mercury in the third house. Again, she is able to bring her creative ideas and insights into form and has a talent for communicating these to others. The power of the voice and the written word is clearly very important to Jen.

A trine between Uranus and Saturn in the twelfth house indicates that Jen taps into her subconscious mind and dreams during her creative process. This trine bestows an innate sense of structure and order, and is useful for helping Jen to organize her ideas so that they are workable and practical. Her humanitarian impulse from Uranus is strong, and with the twelfth house influence there is likely to be a desire to use her creative work in order to put out a positive, caring message to others.

Uranus is in opposition to Chiron in the eleventh house. Jen is able to use her Uranian insights in order to view herself from a fresh perspective when issues come to the fore. She may try to ignore or deny these issues at first and that could result in health problems which act as reminders to pay more attention to her own needs. However, by listening to her body's promptings, Jen is able to intuitively understand what is necessary for her healing process.

Jen's Uranus is square her Ascendant and Descendant. This indicates that her desire for independence could make relationships an issue. She could improve her romantic life by exploring the benefits that can be found in partnership instead of viewing this as something that could hold her back and stop her from expressing herself freely.

Keywords for Jen's recreation and creativity: innovative, creative, inspired, dramatic, resourceful, practical, independent, imaginative, enthusiastic, communicative, humanitarian.

Go back to the notes that you have made on recreation, romance and creativity. By examining your fifth house, Leo, the Sun, the triplicities and quadruplicities, you can understand what forms the foundation for your creative and romantic drives. Exploring the planets and their aspects can help you to further understand the characteristics and qualities that are readily available. This makes it easier for you to discover and develop your creative potential.

Now look at how you can develop your strengths and pinpoint any weaknesses that could be used as the impetus for increased focus, leisure activities and romantic impulses. Consider whether you are giving yourself the necessary time and space for relaxing, having fun, and enjoying life.

RECREATION, ROMANCE AND CREATIVITY SUMMARY:

▶ *the astrological sign on the fifth house*
▶ *triplicity and quadruplicity*
▶ *the ruling planet of the sign on the fifth house*
▶ *position of Leo in birth chart*
▶ *position of the Sun in birth chart*
▶ *planets in the fifth house*
▶ *aspects to planets in the fifth house.*

10 THINGS TO REMEMBER

1 *Your modes of play, recreation and creativity are revealed through the fifth house.*

2 *The fifth house is ruled by Leo and the Sun.*

3 *The fifth house shows the areas in which you shine.*

4 *Your approach to social enjoyment and romance is revealed in the fifth house.*

5 *The fifth house also governs children, and teaching abilities.*

6 *The astrological sign on the fifth house shows how you express your creative, playful energy and gain confidence.*

7 *Planets in the fifth house emphasize how you express yourself in enjoying life.*

8 *Your sense of drama and flair can be explored through the fifth house.*

9 *Aspects to fifth house planets reveal gifts or challenges in your romantic and creative life.*

10 *Your leadership qualities are revealed through the first house, fifth house, Leo and the Sun.*

11

Health and work

In this chapter you will learn:
- *about the physiology of the astrological signs*
- *about exploring health issues through your birth chart*
- *about the type of work which you are most suited to.*

Health

There is an area of astrology called medical astrology, which focuses tightly on health and can be used to pinpoint particular areas of concern and give guidance as to how to maintain your health and find the most appropriate treatment for health problems. This can be very effective, particularly with regard to unusual or chronic complaints but, as with all methods of health advice, should be used in conjunction with regular medical monitoring. However, in this chapter we will look at the overview of your health and how you can use your birth chart to find particular weaknesses or strengths.

Insight

Each of the planets is related to strengths and weaknesses in different areas of your health, and aspects between planets give more detailed information. Challenging aspects to the Sun could mean a potential back or heart weakness, whereas a well-aspected Sun indicates a strong constitution and positive attitude.

The starting point is the sixth house, which is ruled by Virgo and Mercury. Virgo governs health and work, and Virgos reputation is that of being very health-conscious. Diet, exercise and grooming are all of interest to the Virgoan nature and this sign, especially if there are challenging aspects to Mercury, can be prone to nervous complaints, stress-related or diet-related digestive problems and hypochondria. Food allergies or sensitivity are often a challenge to Virgos. By looking at the area of your chart where Virgo is placed, you can see where there is likely to be a focus on your health and diet.

The sixth house reveals particular health issues. The sign on this house can inform you of particular weaknesses and offer pointers as to how you can deal with these. Each astrological sign governs specific areas of the body.

Insight

Each astrological sign rules a part of the body. The sign of your Sun and Ascendant show predispositions towards physical strengths and weaknesses, and the sign on your sixth house can reveal any health issues that you may need to pay extra attention to.

Physiology of astrological signs

Aries rules the head.

Taurus rules the throat.

Gemini rules the lungs and nervous system.

Cancer rules the breasts and stomach.

Leo rules the heart and spine.

Virgo rules the abdomen and digestive system.

Libra rules the kidneys.

Scorpio rules the urinary system and sexual organs.

Sagittarius rules the sciatic nerve, hips and thighs.

Capricorn rules the skeletal system, teeth and bones.

Aquarius rules the calves and ankles.

Pisces rules the feet and emotional sensitivity.

Look at the astrological sign on your sixth house. What does this tell you about the parts of your body that could be subject to strain or weakness?

Planets in the sixth house give more detailed information about strengths and weaknesses regarding your health. Positive aspects between sixth-house planets indicate a healthy flow of energy between the areas of the body involved, whereas challenging aspects reveal areas that could give rise to health issues or potential problems.

The planets and health

Sun: constitution, heart, back and self-esteem.

Moon: emotional issues, breasts, stomach.

Mercury: nervous diseases and chest problems.

Venus: sore throats, loss of voice, kidney problems.

Mars: fevers, headaches, accidents, usually swift recovery.

Jupiter: weight gain issues, gallstones, digestion.

Saturn: teeth, bones, arthritis, depression.

Uranus: sudden onsets, unusual complaints, epilepsy.

Neptune: mysterious illnesses or reactions to medication, drugs or alcohol.

Pluto: reproductive areas, disability and deep-rooted psychological issues.

Chiron: inner wounds, which can have physical, mental or emotional repercussions.

By looking at the planets in your sixth house, and aspects to these, you can find out the most likely health weaknesses and work to strengthen these areas. Complimentary therapies can be of enormous use, especially herbalism as there is a close connection between herbs and astrological rulerships. You can take simple practical steps to avoid problems by paying attention to the area of your body that is most vulnerable. For instance, if you have challenging aspects to Venus in the sixth house, ensure that you keep your throat warm and you can avoid sore throats or loss of your voice. If Mercury has challenging aspects, practise a form of relaxation in order to strengthen your nervous system and avoid stress-related complaints.

> Look at your chart again and note down any planets in the sixth house and their aspects. What does this tell you about your health? Now look at challenging aspects between your other planets. The effects of these can have an impact on your health too, so see whether you can take any steps to strengthen these areas.

Work

The sixth house is especially relevant in terms of service and the type of work through which you feel fulfilled, and can also enable, empower or provide something that can be of use to others. The placement of Virgo also reveals where you are most likely to apply attention to detail and can create and maintain a sense of order.

Career, work and business are viewed as separate areas in your birth chart, although these are likely to be strongly interwoven. For career goals, the tenth house is the area of examination. For business, the second and eighth houses are relevant. For your basic attitudes towards work and the type of work to which you are suited, look at the sixth-house influences.

Your astrological sign predisposes you to certain qualities that influence the type of work you choose and your interests and needs. The sign on the sixth house and planets situated here tell you a great deal about your attitudes and the most suitable and effective working environment.

Insight

The sixth house shows the areas through which you find fulfilment through work, and where you feel that you are also contributing towards the well-being of other people. The sign on the sixth house, and planets within it, show the type of work that is most likely to stimulate you.

The signs and attitudes towards work

Aries needs a challenge and prefers to be a leader.

Taurus has good business sense and staying power.

Gemini has strong communication and networking skills.

Cancer is caring and nurturing towards others.

Leo is magnanimous and enjoys the limelight.

Virgo is practical, perfectionist and helpful.

Libra is sociable and concerned with equality.

Scorpio is focused and good at investigating.

Sagittarius is adventurous and curious.

Capricorn is determined, organized and reliable.

Aquarius is inquisitive, idealistic and humanitarian.

Pisces is caring and intuitive.

Look at your Sun sign and the astrological sign on your sixth house. This will tell you which approach you tend to take towards work and can help you to ascertain the most suitable working environment.

Insight

The astrological sign on the sixth house shows the approach you take towards your work and towards being of service to others. Aries indicates that you throw yourself wholeheartedly into your work, and that you are brimming with new ideas but dislike being bogged down by details.

Planets in the sixth house

Any planets in your sixth house, and aspects that are made to these, can give strong indications of the qualities which can help you to express yourself and feel fulfilled in your area of work.

Sun: you need to feel in charge and to express yourself creatively.

Moon: you need to feel comfortable with co-workers and to have emotional feedback.

Mercury: you need to communicate your ideas and be heard.

Venus: you need harmony and to express your artistic and social skills.

Mars: you need to be active and be in a leadership role.

Jupiter: you need to feel that your knowledge is being broadened.

Saturn: you need to use your organizing skills and have a long-range plan.

Uranus: you need the freedom to express and carry through your ideas.

Neptune: you need to feel a sense of connection and purpose through your work.

Pluto: you need to feel that your work is significant and transformative.

By looking at the planets in your sixth house, and aspects to these, you can discover which qualities will help you to choose work that carries a sense of satisfaction and meaning for you. If this is not present in your current area of work you can look for other work options which would be more fulfilling, or use your birth chart to find ways in which you can make your work situation or environment more effective for your well-being.

Insight

Any planets in the sixth house describe the type of energy that you focus on in order to fully immerse yourself into your chosen area of work. For instance, Mercury indicates that you enjoy communicating and are excellent at people-skills and networking.

Look at any planets in the sixth house and aspects made to these. Consider how you are currently using the qualities associated with these planets and whether you can develop these further. Note your strengths and weaknesses. How can these be improved upon? If you are considering changing your area of work, take into account the information in your birth chart in order to make the most of your skills.

JEN'S CHART

Look back at Jen's chart on page 17. Jen's sixth house is an area of her chart that takes up almost as much space as her much expanded fifth house, so her work and health are extremely important to her. Her sixth house begins with Scorpio but contains all of Sagittarius. This indicates that she needs to feel that there can be a transformative effect through both health and work, and that she can use her learned wisdom and understanding in order to guide others towards utilizing their skills and talents. The Scorpio cusp reveals that she seeks a great deal of inner meaning in this area of life and has immense focus. As Scorpio is the sign of death and regeneration, Jen's health and work situations are likely to experience strong fluctuations while she is becoming established but, like the mythical phoenix, she is able to courageously face challenges and rise above them.

Sagittarius contained within Jen's sixth house shows that she has immense enthusiasm, confidence and optimism regarding her health and work. She needs to feel that she can expand her mind as well as her physical horizons and has an urge to communicate what she has learned to those around her. She is dynamic and determined but is open to being flexible when necessary.

Neptune in the sixth house, in Sagittarius, indicates that Jen is sensitive to medications and is likely to suffer through allergies or mysterious, difficult-to-diagnose ailments. Alcohol could be detrimental to her health. Neptune is square the Moon and Mars. This can indicate loss of energy and feelings of exhaustion because the vitality of Mars is drained by the square aspect. With the Moons involvement there is likely to be an underlying emotional cause to ailments, which manifests subconsciously as tiredness and exhaustion. Through finding the cause of the imbalance, Jen can take steps to increasing her energy levels, which is the first step to recovery from illness.

Jupiter in Sagittarius in the sixth house gives Jen optimism and confidence and prompts her to look for spiritual or philosophical meaning in both her state of health and her work. This position brings an interest in complimentary therapies or holistic methods of healing. She views herself as a whole person rather than in segments and is certain that one aspect of her life affects the rest. This gives her a strong basis for seeking out the modes of healing which will be most effective for her. She also has a strong desire to help others to improve their lives.

Jupiter square Pluto indicates that health issues are deep-rooted and are related to being subjected to an issue or situation of power, dominance or control. Bringing this to the surface in order to deal with it could be painful but would ultimately bring about a state of healing and regeneration, which is likely to be long-lasting.

Chiron, which reveals the inner wound that needs to be healed, is situated in Jen's eleventh house, in Aries, indicating that issues of trust could affect her health. As this is in opposition to Uranus in the fifth house, Jen's health issues are likely to be sudden, unexpected and unusual in nature. This aspect, combined with Jen's Neptune, is a strong pointer to her medical history of ME/CFIDS.

Work is of great importance to Jen. Her Scorpio and Sagittarius sixth house shows that she needs to use her opportunities and to create lasting, positive changes for others as well as for herself through her skills and talents. Her Neptune square Moon and Mars indicates that Jen may feel let down or betrayed in the course of her work but is able eventually to pick up the pieces and move on with a positive attitude. Jen clearly learns from experience, with Jupiter also in this house.

Jupiter in opposition to the Ascendant reveals a reluctance to be tied down and Jen's need for independence could result in missed opportunities. However, Jupiter sextile MC dilutes this somewhat as it indicates that Jen's outgoing, cheerful nature brings a great deal of support that helps to improve her career prospects.

Virgo is on Jen's fourth house. A harmonious home life is important to Jen's health and well-being, and much of her work is likely to take place in her home environment, which she views as her sanctuary and retreat. Jen needs to feel secure and to know that she has a solid foundation and framework in her life. Virgo's ruling planet, Mercury, is situated in her third house, which indicates that communication is the currency in which Jen trades. This is vital to her work and leads her to explore and investigate methods of dealing with health issues. As Mercury is sextile Saturn and Uranus, Jen uses her communication skills effectively yet with care. She ensures that her innovative and unusual ideas are structured and workable before giving voice to them. The trine between Mercury and Chiron reveals that Jen is compelled to share what she has discovered about methods of healing which have been effective for her in the hope that this information will help others.

Jen needs to feel that she can challenge herself and constantly works at improving her skills. Knowledge and training combine with the intuitive qualities of Jen's Neptune and she has a powerful sense of imagery and form. Jen's work as a film-maker is clearly very much in harmony with her birth chart.

Keywords for Jen's health and work: transformative, mysterious, expansive, dynamic, flexible, intuitive, independent, creative, unusual, optimistic, confident.

Return to your notes on health and work. By looking at the astrological sign on the sixth house, planets within it and their aspects, you can understand your strengths, weaknesses and needs. This will enable you to find ways in which you can make the best of your health and talents.

This information can help you to feel more empowered regarding your health and work.

HEALTH AND WORK SUMMARY:

▶ *the astrological sign on the sixth house*
▶ *its triplicity and quadruplicity*
▶ *Virgo and Mercury in birth chart*
▶ *planets in the sixth house*
▶ *aspects to planets in the sixth house*
▶ *Chiron.*

10 THINGS TO REMEMBER

1 *Each astrological sign governs an area of the body, and can indicate strengths and weaknesses in that area.*

2 *The planets can reveal information about health issues.*

3 *The sixth house gives information about your health, and any health concerns or issues.*

4 *The sixth house is ruled by Virgo, a sign which has a reputation for being health-conscious.*

5 *Positive aspects to planets in the sixth house show good health and care of your body.*

6 *Challenging sixth-house aspects can point out potential health issues which are indicated by the planets involved.*

7 *The sixth house also rules the area of work which can bring fulfilment to you.*

8 *The astrological sign on the sixth house indicates particular areas of work and service.*

9 *Planets in the sixth house show tendencies towards gifts and abilities in this area.*

10 *The planetoid Chiron reveals health issues, and its position shows how you deal with these.*

12

....

Relationships and partnerships

In this chapter you will learn:
- *about how other people really see you*
- *about your committed relationships and business partnerships*
- *about the qualities of your ideal partner.*

Relating to others is a primary need as well as an urge. This occurs from the moment of birth (when we are dependent on our mother for survival) through to early childhood (when we learn to co-operate and forge friendships) and adulthood (when we expand this drive to include romantic and work partnerships). Our ability to connect with and relate to those around us assures us of our place in the world and solidifies our sense of self.

Your birth chart can reveal how other people perceive you, how you express your desire for partnership and relationships, and what attracts you in a potential partner. The house that focuses on this area is the seventh house, which begins at your Descendant, directly opposite your Ascendant. Whereas the Ascendant and first house describe how you externalize your personality, the Descendant and seventh house show how others perceive you and how you forge connections with those around you. It deals with your relationship needs and also with business partnerships. Challenging aspects concerning the seventh house can indicate relationship problems, or can mean that you are faced with having to deal with or confront a person (or people) who actively and openly oppose you. Other information that can be gained from this house include legal matters and your sense of justice and fairness.

Before you begin to explore your seventh house, write down your feelings about relationships. You could include the qualities which you are most drawn to in a romantic partner, if you like. It can be useful to see how these notes compare with what you find when you look at the relationship information in your chart.

The seventh house is governed by Libra and Venus. Libra deals with partnerships, with matters of love, with harmony, legal issues, your sense of justice, and enemies or adversaries who are known to you. Venus is the planet of love, harmony, artistic and musical talents, and beauty. The astrological sign on your seventh house reveals your public persona, how you appear to other people, and gives information about what you look for in relationships, how you conduct yourself and whether you are more comfortable with a degree of independence or need a close partnership in order to feel fulfilled. The triplicity and quadruplicity of your seventh house sign indicates your mode of expression within relationships.

The signs and relationships

Aries: you need romance and stimulation.

Taurus: you need loving touch and stability.

Gemini: you need friendship and communication.

Cancer: you need security and nurturing.

Leo: you need positive feedback and romance.

Virgo: you need practical demonstrations of affection.

Libra: you need reciprocation and to be an equal partner.

Scorpio: you need passion and intensity.

Sagittarius: you need intellectual stimulation.

Capricorn: you need security and commitment.

Aquarius: you need independence and friendship.

Pisces: you need cherishing and thoughtfulness.

> Look at the sign on your seventh house. Explore the characteristics, triplicity and quadruplicity of that sign and, together with the brief sentence given about the signs and relationships, write down some keywords about your attitude towards relationships.

As the natural rulers of the seventh house are Libra and Venus, look at where these are placed in your birth chart. The house which Libra is situated over and the sign and house in which Venus is placed can give you a great deal of information. The house over which Libra is found reveals the area of life in which you most strongly express your need for relationships and partnership. If Libra is on your sixth house, for instance, work partnerships and the possibility of meeting a significant romantic partner through your work is likely. Libra on the ninth house can indicate that you meet your partner while travelling or far from home or that your partner is from a different culture.

Your Venus placement shows how you express your artistic talents and need for harmony, and also reveals how you express yourself in relationships. Venus governs the need to give and receive love and affection. If Venus is in Taurus, you will be immensely sensual, tactile and romantic, with a desire for pleasure and for giving and receiving gifts. Venus in Aquarius reveals that you like to be friends with everyone and that friendship is as important as romance. You will need to keep a degree of independence in relationships and are not likely to wish to be bound to the traditional view of relationships. The house placement of Venus indicates the area of life through which your affections are most strongly exhibited. In the first house, for instance, your charming, easy-going nature will win you many friends and admirers, and you are likely to be fascinated by love and to strongly desire partnerships.

Your potential partner

In a man's chart, the position of Venus indicates the type of romantic partner to whom he is attracted. For instance, Venus in Libra shows that you are naturally attracted to someone who is sociable, easy-going, demonstrative and who takes care of their appearance. Venus in the fifth house reveals that you will be drawn to a partner who is romantic, outgoing and creative, and who enjoys having fun.

In a woman's chart, the position of Mars indicates the type of romantic partner to whom she is attracted. Mars in Sagittarius, for instance, indicates that you are attracted to someone who is active, energetic and mentally stimulating. Mars in the eighth house shows that you will be drawn to a partner who is intense and passionate, with hidden depths.

Study the placement of Venus if you are male and Mars if you are female. Consider any relationships you have had. Did these fit with the emotional needs that are described in your birth chart? By understanding what you subconsciously look for in a relationship, you can increase your opportunities for romantic happiness.

Next, look at any planets in the seventh house. These, and any aspects made to them, will give more information about your self-expression within relationships and partnerships, and will tell you a great deal about the nature of your relationships. If there are several planets in the seventh house, this indicates that there is a strong focus on relationships and partnerships.

Insight

Any planets in the seventh house, along with the position of Venus in a man's chart and Mars in a woman's chart, give information about the type of partner whom you are most attracted to. You can choose to develop these qualities to increase opportunities for a fulfilling relationship.

Business partnerships

The likelihood of business partnerships or collaborations is also shown in the seventh house. Again, look at the astrological sign on the cusp, any planets within this house and aspects made to them. If you are already involved in a partnership, it can be useful to have both partners' charts before you and to compare what is in each chart for a detailed view of the energies that are predominant in the partnership.

Planets in the seventh house

Sun: romantic, easy-going, fair.

Moon: committed, emotional, demonstrative.

Mercury: sociable, co-operative, communicative.

Venus: loving, warm, harmonious.

Mars: dynamic, forthcoming, competitive.

Jupiter: generous, optimistic, confident.

Saturn: responsible, enduring, serious.

Uranus: exciting, independent, unusual.

Neptune: intuitive, emotional, idealistic.

Pluto: perceptive, intense, transformative.

Chiron: balanced, instructive, compassionate.

> **Insight**
> Seventh-house planets, and any aspects to these, reveal
> the main energy that you bring to relationships. Venus
> would indicate that you are loving and demonstrative,
> and prefer relationships which are caring and harmonious.

Forging relationships

The sign on your seventh house, any planets situated there, their
aspects and the position of Venus, all reveal your needs and self-
expression in relationships. Through understanding what type
of partner and relationship will be most compatible for you,
relationships can be more harmonious. The information in your
birth chart can also help you to follow your personal path in forging
new relationships. By looking at the factors in your birth chart,
you can gauge whether you are making the most of your potential
to connect with other people. If, for instance, you are a confirmed
romantic, with Venus in the seventh house, you can choose to

develop your positive qualities in order to attract a potential partner. The characteristics that are visible in your chart are all 'potentials', which means that it is up to you whether you choose to develop these or leave them in the background. Your chart can be used as a tool for self-empowerment as well as character analysis and guidance.

> Look at the notes you have made and write a list of what you consider to be your relationship needs, hopes, strengths and weaknesses. Look at the notes you have made on what you unconsciously seek in a potential partner. Think about how you can work constructively with these so that you maximize your potential and possibilities. How can you improve on your strengths and work with any weaknesses?

Insight

You can use the information within your seventh house to enhance your relationships. If challenging aspects are present you can use these as a tool for self-analysis, and focus on your strong points. Positive aspects can help you to make the most of your ability to connect with others.

JEN'S CHART

Look back at Jen's chart on page 17. Jen's seventh house is in Capricorn, which is a cardinal earth sign. This shows that Jen is practical about relationships and, when committed, gives a great deal of herself. It is likely that her long-term partner will be older than herself as the maturity of the Capricorn nature tends to seek out others who are also mature and responsible.

Venus is in Cancer in the twelfth house. Despite Jen's apparently outgoing nature, evident in other factors of her chart, she has a shy side and finds it hard to open up to strangers. Venus in Cancer indicates that Jen would find it hard, even impossible, to make the first move if she is attracted to someone. She needs time to get to know and trust her potential partner and can be insecure in relationships. However, once she has opened up she is loving, warm, compassionate and demonstrative, and enjoys caring for her partner. The home is viewed as a 'safe space' and Jen is likely to show her feelings through cooking and nurturing more easily than through ardent, open demonstrations of love.

Venus conjunct the Ascendant shows that others find Jen charming and attractive, and this brings many opportunities for love and romance. She is easy-going, friendly and seeks harmony. Once she has committed herself to a friendship, partnership or relationship, she allows her inner self to shine through and tends to feel that connections in her life will be long-lasting and mutually supportive.

Jen's Venus opposition Jupiter in the sixth house indicates that Jen is sweet-natured and benevolent but with a love of the good things of life that can make her too laid-back or extravagant at times. She enjoys making herself attractive and views this almost as a game, not to be taken too seriously.

A square between Venus and Pluto in the fourth house reveals that Jen's trusting nature could be abused, which would lead to a period of emotional withdrawal. Jen's innate optimism and positivity can help her to bounce back once her emotions have had time to settle.

Venus is trine Jen's MC, which indicates that her creative abilities bring her career success in the arts. This aspect also means that a partnership and romantic relationship are likely to come through Jen's career.

Mars in Leo in the third house shows that Jen's most compatible potential partner is someone who is creative, sociable, outgoing and confident. She needs a partner who is an Alpha figure, a strong leader, and who she can have fun with and possibly share creative interests with. Communication is an important factor for Jen in partnerships.

There are no planets in Jen's seventh house and the area of her chart which is taken up by this is small in comparison with other houses. This reveals that, for Jen, love and romance do not take top priority in her life. However, once emotionally involved, her Capricorn house sign ensures that she is steadfast and committed.

Keywords for Jen's relationships and partnerships: earthy, committed, shy, caring, loving, harmonious, optimistic, older partner, trusting, compassionate.

Return to the notes that you have made on relationships and partnerships. By looking at your seventh house, Venus, the triplicities and quadruplicities, you can understand your inner needs and drives. By exploring the planets and aspects, you can gain a great deal of information about how you express yourself in relationships. This can help you to foster harmonious partnerships with those you are closely involved with. Looking at the position of Mars gives information on your ideal partner if you are a woman. For a man, looking at the position of Venus tells you about the type of woman who is most suited to you in a relationship.

Now look again at your perceived strengths and weaknesses. How can you make these into positive attributes? If your chart reveals that you are shy about making new connections, you can work on gradually building your confidence. If you have found relationships difficult, your chart can help you to see which characteristics and qualities you should be looking for in order to find the right partner for you.

RELATIONSHIPS AND PARTNERSHIPS SUMMARY:

▶ *the astrological sign on the seventh house*
▶ *triplicity and quadruplicity*
▶ *ruling planet of the seventh-house sign*
▶ *planets in the seventh house*
▶ *aspects to these planets*
▶ *Mars for women to see the ideal male attributes*
▶ *Venus for men to see the ideal female attributes.*

10 THINGS TO REMEMBER

1 *The seventh house is concerned with relationships, marriage and business partnerships.*

2 *The Descendant is directly opposite your Ascendant, and shows how others perceive you.*

3 *The seventh house is ruled by Libra and Venus.*

4 *The astrological sign on your seventh house reveals your approach to relationships.*

5 *The triplicity and quadruplicity of your seventh house indicates your attitudes to and within relationships.*

6 *Planets in the seventh house reveal the types of relationships that you engage in, and the qualities that attract you.*

7 *The position of Venus in a male chart and Mars in a female chart shows the qualities that you are drawn to in a partner.*

8 *Harmony or stresses in business partnerships are shown through the sign on the seventh house, and planets placed there.*

9 *You can discover much information about partnerships and relationships through exploring the sign, planets and aspects connected to the seventh house.*

10 *Aspects to Venus in any area of your chart give further information about your love relationships.*

13

....

Financial matters and regenerative powers

In this chapter you will learn:
- *about your approach to finances and your deep inner resources*
- *about your ability to regenerate*
- *about issues which you consider and question deeply.*

In your birth chart, financial matters are looked at as an adjunct to your earning power and attitude towards possessions, which take a highly personal perspective in the second house. Finances include resources such as stocks and bonds, shared or distributed wealth, inheritance, taxes, insurance, corporate finance and money that concerns or belongs to others. The management of your resources and the exchange of these resources, which takes place in a businesslike manner, is the focal point of this area of your chart.

When there is an exchange of energy, whether this is financial or in any other form such as plans or goods, this necessitates an interchange of energy between both parties involved. In essence a relationship is created, whether this is for commercial or other reasons, and the interplay of energy and communication between the people involved creates the foundation and framework on which the 'business' can take place. If you view your birth chart as a progression, your capacity for forging relationships and partnerships in the seventh house acts as a springboard for your ability to make business connections and follow these through.

The area of your birth chart that provides this information is the eighth house. This reveals your deep inner resources, your primal drives and significant financial matters. The eighth house, which is ruled by Scorpio, Mars and Pluto, also shows your attitudes towards sex, danger and death, and reveals how and through which avenue you go through the processes of releasing and renewing or regenerating.

> **Insight**
>
> Money and resources are a form of energy that only have value when they can be exchanged for what you need or desire. The eighth house shows how you feel about, and work with, the resources which are available to you.

Scorpio is the most intense astrological sign. It is deep, secretive, mysterious and concerned with exploring and investigating what lies beneath the surface of everyday things. Sex, finance and death are primal drives, closely bound through the natural urge to regenerate, to accumulate and speculate in order to increase the chances of surviving and to release what is no longer necessary in order to start afresh.

Mars is associated with your energy, motivation and drive, with courage and leadership. Its position reveals the area where you exhibit your warrior traits. Pluto is associated with resourcefulness, depth, introversion, control, obsession and with the desire to go to the root of matters in order to understand the truth, which can be found through investigating the source. In mythology, Pluto is the god of the Underworld, where souls were taken after death, and is also the god of wealth and hidden treasures. This planet, named after the deity, is an apt ruler of the eighth house.

> **Insight**
>
> The eighth house is ruled by the astrological sign Scorpio, and the planets Mars and Pluto. These all embody a strong degree of emotional intensity, strength and courage, which is reflected in the ability for deep thought and resourcefulness that you can access, whatever situation you may find yourself in.

The matters under the rulership of the eighth house can be viewed as your testing ground, the area in which you deal with sometimes difficult challenges and undergo a transformation through facing them. Dealing with finances that are concerned with, or generated through, others is a responsibility which, especially in the arena of large-scale finance, can be life-changing for good or ill. Facing the fact of your mortality can be a painful and frightening experience, but ultimately leads to acceptance and the desire to live life as fully as possible, to understand it, to question who you are and why you are here. Letting go of cherished attachments, whether these are in the form of material things or people, is not an easy process, yet is an unavoidable part of life. Through that releasing process something new can emerge. Death leads to regeneration. These are the fundamental keynotes for the eighth house.

Insight

The eighth house governs finances and resources. The sign on your eighth house shows your approach to, and attitudes towards, finances. Aries stimulates you to speculate and take risks, whereas Capricorn indicates patience and the ability to save and spend wisely.

The sign on the eighth house, its triplicity and quadruplicity can tell you immediately how you express yourself in these areas of life.

The signs on the eighth house and finance

Aries: you are a risk-taker, ready to leap at challenges.

Taurus: you have sound business and financial sense, and invest cautiously.

Gemini: you are speculative and versatile, needing to have several options to hand.

Cancer: you hold tightly to what you have and may inherit money or real-estate.

Leo: you are generous and can be over-extravagant.

Virgo: you worry easily about finance but are reliable and steady.

Libra: you may gain through partnership but tend to spend on luxuries.

Scorpio: you acquire wealth through your ability to understand those in power.

Sagittarius: you are free-spending and philosophical about finances.

Capricorn: you accumulate through your resourcefulness and patience.

Aquarius: you are altruistic and interested in shared resources.

Pisces: you worry about joint finances but find materialistic values distasteful.

> Look at the sign on your eighth house and at its triplicity and quadruplicity. What immediately springs to mind about how these indicate your attitudes towards financial matters, your deep inner resources, sex and death? Note these down.
>
> The natural rulers of the eighth house are Mars and Pluto. By looking at their positions in your birth chart, you can see the areas in which you most actively express your desires. Look also at the position of Scorpio in your birth chart. The house on which it is situated will reveal the area of life through which you can most effectively increase your financial status and work with your powers of transformation and regeneration.

Planets in your eighth house reveal how you express and fulfil your needs and desires. As the eighth house governs the desire principle in all its forms, planets found here will have a profound impact on how you view financial matters and how you go about fulfilling your curiosity about matters that are meaningful to you through exploration and investigation. The curiosity of the eighth house is focused on issues that you consider to be deep and vital, rather than being directed superficially. For instance, Aries on the eighth house with Mars situated within it will manifest as a do-or-die attitude, immense courage and a tendency to jump in where angels fear to tread. You are likely to be accident prone because you leap first and think later and you will have no fear of physical harm or even death, which would be viewed as just another adventure. Financially you will be a risk-taker and prone to get-rich-quick schemes or speculation as you follow the impulses of the moment rather than projecting thoughts about consequences in the future. If you lose a deal you will shrug your shoulders and move on. A high sex drive and a love of the chase will bring the likelihood of passionate encounters and others will find you attractive, though sometimes too forceful.

Planets in the eighth house

Sun: strong-willed, questioning, dominating, intense.

Moon: sensitive, alluring, possessive, emotionally manipulative.

Mercury: penetrating, secretive, compelling, investigatory.

Venus: sensual, possessive, regenerative, changeable.

Mars: passionate, courageous, risk-taker, accident-prone.

Jupiter: deep-thinking, mystery-oriented, curious, inherited wealth.

Saturn: businesslike, investing, responsible, private.

Uranus: intuitive, insightful, changeable finances, penetrating.

Neptune: intuitive, transcendental, manipulative, mysterious.

Pluto: intense, passionate, willpower, accumulated wealth.

Chiron: resourceful, exploratory, mystical, quiet.

> **Insight**
> Planets situated in the eighth house, and aspects to these,
> give a great deal of information about your use of resources.
> These may be financial, or the resources deep within you that
> you can call upon in order to overcome challenges or start
> afresh in an area of your life.

Increasing your regenerative capacity

Your capacity for regeneration can be called on through exploring
the sign on the eighth house and planets within it. Your birth chart
shows your potential, so you can work with any factor in your
chart in order to expand its sphere of influence and fulfil whichever
possibilities occur to you.

When you look at the characteristics and qualities of your eighth-
house influence, this reveals particular strengths and weaknesses.
Note these down and look at other factors in your birth chart
to see how you can use your inner resources more effectively.
For instance, if Pluto is in the second house in your chart, with
square aspects to it, this can indicate that your income and earning
power are subject to change and upheaval. Your fear of losing
what you have may make you try to hold on grimly to it, risking
damage to relationships. In this case, you can intentionally use the
determination and innate earning power of Pluto by looking at how
you can be more resourceful. Going deep into the reasons for why you
seek to hold on to financial gain can help you to understand your
needs and can show you how you can balance this out in order to
meet your root needs while being aware that change can be used
for your growth rather than as a cause of great concern.

Insight

The eighth house shows how you can tap into your inner resources, especially during difficult times. The house position, and aspects to Pluto in your birth chart reveal the areas in which you experience the need to regenerate or start afresh in order to bring about inner and outer transformation.

JEN'S CHART

Look back at Jen's chart on page 17. Jen's eighth house begins with Capricorn, a cardinal earth sign. She is practical, careful and sensible about her financial dealings and is likely to invest wisely and look to the long term. As her eighth house also includes Aquarius, the combination of these two astrological signs reveals that Jen has a deep interest in metaphysical subjects that take a scientific approach, such as astrology and quantum healing. The practical application of systems that explore energy and the nature of reality, such as the principles of quantum physics and the use of visualization techniques, are of interest to Jen, but must bear tangible results in order to maintain her interest. The Aquarian side of her eighth house indicates that her energy flow fluctuates, but the Capricorn side shows that she has a great deal of tenacity and perseverance and has strong powers of recuperation and a robust approach. She tends to worry about making her finances work effectively, but is resilient and able to keep motivated and to determinedly regenerate after challenging times.

Saturn, the ruler of Capricorn, is in Gemini in the twelfth house, with a trine to Uranus and sextile to Chiron in the eleventh house. In terms of Jen's financial matters and powers of regeneration, this shows that she is good at managing financial partnerships involving others, especially those that involve innovative avenues of income and investment. The Chiron sextile reveals an altruistic streak. Jen seeks to reward those who make an effort and has a humanitarian outlook. Jen has a strong survival instinct and is capable of great endurance and perseverance, combined with the ability to explore alternative ideas when matters are not progressing as she hopes.

As Saturn and Uranus are co-rulers of Aquarius, the qualities described above are also directed into her creative abilities and it is likely that her financial status will be elevated through the trading of new and unusual ideas. Jen works well with others and enjoys the exchange of information, ideas and inspiration. This, combined with her natural optimism, helps her to forge strong, lasting partnerships.

Scorpio is on Jen's fifth house, which indicates that Jen's strongest resources come through her creativity and her ability to be a natural leader. The playful qualities of the fifth house are taken seriously by Jen in the sense that she views creativity, play and the dramatic side of her nature as being her path to deep understanding and knowledge of her craft. Jen may well feel that this fundamental element of her life is 'meant to be' and is her destiny.

Mars and Pluto, rulers of Scorpio, are respectively in the third and fourth house. Jen uses her communication skills effectively and dynamically in order to ascertain and increase financial acumen, and needs the solid framework of a home base as a backdrop to projecting herself out into the world. Pluto is trine the North node, which is situated in Jen's eighth house. This shows that Jen has a very powerful insight into, and awareness of, the fashions and trends that are current and which are about to emerge. She taps into these insights and uses her charisma to further her goals. This aspect indicates a revolutionary attitude and Jen is likely to transform the ideas and concepts of others. She could become renowned for her work because she expresses awareness of a deeper purpose than merely financial gain. Jen takes a spiritual perspective and views all interactions as an exchange of energy, which can be used to enhance the lives of those involved.

Keywords for Jen's financial matters and regenerative power: practical, sensible, survival instincts, determined, persevering, private, resourceful, insightful, collaborative, sense of destiny.

Return to your notes on financial matters and regenerative power. By looking at the sign on your eighth house, its triplicity, quadruplicity and ruling planet, and Scorpio, Mars and Pluto, you can understand the forces that form the foundation and can be used as a springboard. By exploring the planets in the eighth house and how these indicate your needs and drives, you can see which qualities will be most helpful to you.

FINANCIAL MATTERS AND REGENERATIVE POWERS SUMMARY:

- ▶ *the astrological sign on the eighth house*
- ▶ *its triplicity and quadruplicity*
- ▶ *its ruling planet(s)*
- ▶ *the ruling planet of the sign on the eighth house*
- ▶ *the position of Scorpio in birth chart*
- ▶ *the position of Mars and Pluto*
- ▶ *planets in the eighth house*
- ▶ *aspects to planets in the eighth house.*

10 THINGS TO REMEMBER

1 *There is a link between the second house of possessions and the eighth house of finances.*

2 *The eighth house reveals information about your deep resources.*

3 *The eighth house is ruled by Scorpio, Mars and Pluto.*

4 *Any issues involving personal power and control can be highlighted by the eighth-house position.*

5 *The sign on the eighth-house cusp reveals your mode of expression in finance and resources.*

6 *Your capacity for starting afresh and coping with change and upheaval is shown through the eighth house.*

7 *Planets in the eighth house reveal how you experience and achieve your desires.*

8 *The eighth house gives information about strengths and weaknesses which can help or hinder situations involving change.*

9 *The eighth house is associated with other people's money or resources, such as taxes, wills and inheritances.*

10 *Looking at Pluto's position in your chart reveals your potent use of the will and resources.*

14

....

Further education and travel

In this chapter you will learn:
- *about your attitudes towards further education and developing knowledge*
- *about travel possibilities*
- *about how to create more opportunities for growth.*

The term 'further education' applies to any form of exploration, gathering of information and knowledge that goes beyond the basics of the accepted view of general primary and secondary school education. This may take the form of college or university, of involvement in courses that interest you, of an interest in developing aspects of yourself or through a deep sense of curiosity about the world, humanity, philosophy or religion. The opportunities for further education are multiple because we are constantly learning, developing and growing.

In your birth chart, the third house deals with communication and with relationships and personal connections that involve those such as siblings, neighbours, friends and acquaintances. Third-house communication takes place through the development of curiosity as a means of beginning to make sense of the world, and through learning that mental stimulation is the foundation for learning and discovery. The third house also deals with early education. It reveals our aptitude for learning and indicates any issues or challenges that either distract from this or can hinder us in the learning process. The factors in your third house form the springboard for the further education that takes place as we mature. The impulse to question and to seek answers, which enable a broader view of life, comes into play in the ninth house. While the key phrase for the third house is 'I think', the key phrase for the ninth house moves outwards and externalizes into 'I explore'.

The ninth house deals with communication on a wide-ranging scale. From the innate curiosity of the third house, which is geared towards finding out who you are through interactions with others, the mind expands and reaches out in the ninth house to enquire about and encompass your interrelationships, community, culture and humanity, and to find a framework for philosophical questions.

Insight

The ninth house and Jupiter are concerned with communication over distances. This can take the form of travel to other countries, or study that stimulates philosophical thought and broadens the horizons of your mind.

One element of the ninth house is tradition. Religion, philosophy, law, publishing and teaching are all areas that are governed by rules that we are expected to accept and abide by in order to maintain the status quo. Later, in Chapter 16, we will look at how you strive to go beyond these boundaries in your search for meaning. The main focus of the ninth house is the expansion of your mind and horizons, and how you accomplish this; that expansion can include long-distance travel as a way through which you can learn first-hand about the world. Another method of expressing the expansive qualities of the ninth house is through teaching – a way of using the knowledge you have gained in order to help to expand the minds of others. The keynotes are the gathering and dissemination of meaningful information.
The natural rulers of the ninth house are Sagittarius and Jupiter. The Sagittarian mind is active and enquiring, open and intelligent. Subtlety is not one of the Sagittarian attributes – this sign is

concerned with the truth and is as straightforward and direct as the arrow that characterizes the sign's glyph. Morality, ethics and insight are the key qualities and the goal is expansion through action. Thinking is a serious process for this sign, which focuses on seeking out and exploring new horizons, yet tradition is viewed as a mainstay and strongly-held opinions are not open to debate.

Jupiter, named after the leader of the Roman gods, is the ruling planet. Wisdom, optimism, confidence and good fortune are associated with this planet, along with expansion in all its forms. The planet Jupiter is the largest in our solar system and its orbit has a powerful influence on sunspot cycles, which in turn affect weather systems on Earth. Though far distant, its influence is wide-reaching and an understanding of Jupiter's cycles brings an understanding of the interwoven connections within the vastness of the cosmos. This corresponds with the expansive nature of the ninth house, Sagittarius and Jupiter, which are geared towards the process of gathering and disseminating knowledge.

Insight

Jupiter is the ruling planet of Sagittarius and the ninth house. This is the planet of generosity, benevolence, growth and expansion, and its influence can be physical, philosophical and spiritual.

Look at your birth chart and see where Sagittarius and Jupiter are placed. What does this tell you about how and where you seek to expand your horizons? These areas can indicate your path to further education and interests that help to broaden your mind.

The astrological sign on the ninth house, its triplicity and quadruplicity give information about how you experience and express your desire to learn. It shows the avenues through which you reach out beyond your immediate horizons and seek to increase your knowledge. A strong emphasis on the ninth house in your chart, with planets situated within it, reveals a strong influx of energy that needs to be directed. It tells you even more about how you fulfil your desire to explore the reaches of the mind or how you use travel as a way of increasing your knowledge.

The signs on the ninth house

Aries: you are highly motivated, energetic and a crusader.

Taurus: you are persistent and practical, with social insight and strong views.

Gemini: you are curious, versatile, communicative and likely to travel widely.

Cancer: you are emotional about your philosophies and have an affinity with water.

Leo: you are goal-oriented, philosophical and enjoy travelling.

Virgo: you are consistent and apply yourself rigorously. Research is attractive to you.

Libra: you seek harmony and travel for pleasure. Other cultures are attractive to you.

Scorpio: you have strongly held views and are a religious/philosophical crusader.

Sagittarius: you are traditional, inquisitive, philosophical and stimulating.

Capricorn: you are conservative, concerned and practical in your studies.

Aquarius: you are progressive, rebellious, unconventional and are likely to travel widely.

Pisces: your explorations are religious and mystical and you have a love of the sea.

Insight

The astrological sign on your ninth house indicates how you reach out to gather information that you can use for your personal growth and understanding. Cancer on the ninth house indicates that you feel deeply about your beliefs. Aquarius on the ninth house indicates that you are an independent free-thinker.

Planets in the ninth house reveal how you develop wisdom and knowledge, and how you seek to fulfil your need for exploration, inspiration and discovery. Your social conscience and your desire to pass on what you have learned can be seen in the characteristics and qualities of planets situated in the ninth house. Particular interests in, and approaches to further education and the desire to seek out new horizons through travel can be seen through planets and their aspects in this area.

Planets in the ninth house

Sun: dynamic, spiritual, philosophical, cultural interests, creative intelligence.

Moon: inherited moral and philosophical values, sensitive, intuitive.

Mercury: higher education, immense curiosity, travelling, teaching/lecturing/writing.

Venus: partnership through education, religion, philosophy, creative interests.

Mars: adventurous, needs stimulation, social reformer, outspoken.

Jupiter: energetic, curious, knowledge-seeker, optimistic, much travel, philosophical.

Saturn: traditional, conventional, educationally ambitious, goal-oriented.

Uranus: broad-minded, eccentric, rebellious, idealistic, humanitarian.

Neptune: insightful, intuitive, spiritual, inspirational, abstract mind.

Pluto: transformer, spiritual/philosophical, driven, passionate, uncompromising.

Chiron: higher study, philosophy, keen mind, teaching/lecturing.

Insight

Any planets in the ninth house, and aspects to these, reveal your methods for acquiring knowledge, and show your attitudes to further education. They also show how you expand your mental and physical horizons and explore your interests.

Creating opportunities

The sign on, and planets within, the ninth house and the placement of Sagittarius and Jupiter can be explored in order to see what interests you and how you can develop these interests in order to increase your knowledge and share this with others. By looking at these you can gain insights into how you can work with your potential more effectively. Opportunities for travel can also be explored through these placements and you can see whether you prefer to travel as a pleasurable activity or whether this is necessitated through your studies or work.

For instance, Libra on the ninth house or Venus within the ninth house can indicate that you meet your romantic partner through higher studies, religious or philosophical connections or while abroad. It can also mean that your partner may be met in your homeland but is from a different culture. Your learning process needs to be pleasurable, so you could ensure that any studies you embark on have plenty of scope for creative input.

Look at your chart and note down some keywords that describe the sign on your ninth house, the placements of Sagittarius and Jupiter, planets in the ninth house and any aspects made to these. What does this tell you about your urge to seek information and gain knowledge? How can you use this to broaden your horizons? Consider your perceived strengths and weaknesses. How can you work with these so that they become part of your learning adventures?

Insight

You can use the information given by your ninth house to discover how to take up any opportunities that arise. By looking at the position of Jupiter you can find the areas in which you feel 'lucky' and experience goodwill to and from others.

JEN'S CHART

Look back at Jen's chart on page 17. Aquarius, a fixed air sign, is on Jen's ninth house. This indicates that Jen is immensely curious and enjoys travel as a way of making connections with interesting people and ideas, and also of strengthening connections she has already made. Her approach to higher learning is unconventional and she finds it hard to see the point in following traditions purely because they exist. She is a ground-breaker and innovator, and needs to explore new ideas and fresh horizons as a way of satisfying her diverse interests. Boredom is an alien concept to Jen because everything interests her and she is more likely to feel that there is so much to see, learn, experience and do that there is never enough time to pursue all the things that fascinate her. Her further education needs to be stimulating and allow her to make her own rules and express her independent spirit. Jen's innate optimism and cheerful attitude wins her many friends and colleagues from around the world and helps her to make the most of any opportunities that come her way. Particular areas of further study are those through which she can exchange views and share knowledge, and which appeal to her unusual way of viewing the world. She is very much a 'people person' and is drawn to activities that take place through gatherings of groups of people with common interests. A strong humanitarian streak may prompt a desire to reform existing conditions and make these more broad reaching and palatable for others who lack the opportunities which she has been given.

The ruling planet of Aquarius is Uranus, which is in Libra in Jen's fifth house. Jen expresses her desire to learn through exploring her creative independence and through her humanitarian instincts and impulses. She uses play as a way of learning and furthers her education most easily when the process is fun and appeals to her sense of drama and love of the eccentric, unusual and innovative. The opposition between Uranus and Chiron in the eleventh house reveals that sudden or unusual health issues may cause frustrating delays but that she maintains her connections with others and is still able to retain her sense of excitement about learning something new, especially where groups of people are involved. The square between Uranus and the Ascendant emphasizes Jen's determination to assert her individuality and to make an impact in the fields that interest her. Jen's enjoyment of collaboration is at its height when she feels she has the freedom to explore her ideas and put these in motion.

Jupiter is in Sagittarius, its ruling sign, in Jen's sixth house. Her work means a great deal to her and provides her with a sense of being able to use her knowledge and understanding for the benefit of others. Jen is cheerful and optimistic, with a keen intelligence and a desire to discover all she can about the subjects that catch her attention. Travel is likely to occur mostly in connection with Jen's work and brings about many interesting and stimulating experiences, which Jen is eager to make use of. Jupiter square

Pluto indicates that Jen likes to bring others around to understand her point of view and perspective, and she can be an immovable object if challenged about something that she believes in deeply. Jupiter opposition Ascendant shows that Jen can learn a lot and benefit from partnerships with others but she needs to find ways in which she can still retain some independence. If Jen feels that she is being stifled or dictated to, she is likely to rebel. Jupiter sextile the MC indicates career success and the fulfilment of Jen's goals and ambitions. Others respect her knowledge and opinions, and are keen to co-operate with her. Jen's easy manner and habit of encouraging those around her brings support and opportunities, which add to her status and success. It is likely that Jen's work will make her wealthy and others view her as an inspirational and motivational force.

There are no planets in Jen's ninth house.

Keywords for Jen's further education and travel: intelligent, curious, innovative, unusual, humanitarian, optimistic, confident, respected, independent, rebellious, travel for work.

> Return to your notes on further education and travel. By looking at the sign on your ninth house, its triplicity, quadruplicity and ruling planet, and Sagittarius and Jupiter, you can understand how you express your impulse for learning and how this can be used to increase your potential and develop specific gifts and talents. This will also indicate the likelihood of long-distance travel prospects and shows the ways through which you seek to expand yourself in all areas.

FURTHER EDUCATION AND TRAVEL SUMMARY:

- ▶ *the astrological sign on the ninth house*
- ▶ *its triplicity and quadruplicity*
- ▶ *its ruling planet(s) and their aspects*
- ▶ *position of Sagittarius in birth chart*
- ▶ *position of Jupiter in birth chart.*

10 THINGS TO REMEMBER

1 *The ninth house is ruled by Sagittarius and Jupiter.*

2 *Whereas the third house governs early education, the ninth house governs further education and the pursuit of knowledge.*

3 *Further education includes any form of information-gathering and also the desire to pass on knowledge and explore traditions.*

4 *The key phrase for the ninth house is 'I explore'.*

5 *Travel to other areas and countries is indicated through the ninth-house position.*

6 *The ninth-house sign and planets reveal how you can best expand your mental and physical horizons.*

7 *The astrological sign on the ninth house shows how you experience and pursue learning.*

8 *Planets within the ninth house indicate how you accumulate knowledge and wisdom.*

9 *Aspects to ninth-house planets show easy flow or challenges in pursuing knowledge.*

10 *The placement of Jupiter in your chart indicates how you can make the most of opportunities.*

15

Goals and career

In this chapter you will learn:
- *about your hopes, aims and goals*
- *about your career*
- *about your public persona.*

We all have aims and goals, regardless of their magnitude. These spur us on, keep us vibrant, passionate and hopeful, and keep us motivated. Whether you are single-minded in the pursuit of these, or whether you prefer to meander towards them, taking in other experiences along the way, this can be seen in your birth chart. Your attitudes towards authority, your staying power, your career and the possibility of prominence, celebrity or notoriety can be deciphered through the interpretation of your birth chart.

The tenth house reveals your public persona, the 'you' whom people see from a distance or from a professional perspective. It describes your aims and goals, your career potential and your pinnacle of practical, tangible achievement and is situated at the highest point in your chart. This house contains the Midheaven, the MC and, in the Placidus system which we are using in this book, the MC marks the beginning of the tenth house.

The astrological sign on your tenth house, and its triplicity and quadruplicity, indicate the means through which you seek to reach the heights and achieve your goals, the pinnacle of your particular mountain. The tenth house governs your public persona, your aims, hopes, achievements and area of success. The fourth house, your roots, provides the foundation, which acts as a stepping stone, much as the foundations of a house must be built and the walls erected before the roof can be laid. Directly opposite, in the tenth house, are the indications of the goals and achievements that were conceived in the fourth house. Here can be found your public standing and professional reputation, your vocation as well as your career, and your methods in dealing with power structures and authority. If planets in the tenth house are afflicted with challenging aspects, this reveals the likelihood of disappointment in reaching your goals, or of adverse publicity and notoriety.

For instance, Gemini on your tenth house reveals that you are versatile and need change and stimulation in order to enjoy your career. Your goals may change several times and you may be successful in more than one career. You are a strong, convincing communicator and tend to draw others into your plans. You like progression to be swift because slow progress makes you bored and you lose interest. All areas of communication attract you and your chosen career, and potential for prominence is likely to involve using this skill to its fullest. Writing and public speaking come naturally to you and you thrive on attention and the sharing of ideas. You are an entrepreneur and are always willing to step outside the box and explore ideas from a new angle.

Insight

How you define and accomplish your goals is revealed through the tenth house and through any planets near, and aspects made to, the Midheaven. This area indicates your public persona. It informs you of which characteristics and qualities are publicly noticed, and reveals your potential for success and recognition.

The signs on the tenth house

Aries: you are impatient to succeed, work hard and are impulsive.

Taurus: you value luxury and desire wealth and its accoutrements.

Gemini: you are original, may have more than one career and prominence is likely.

Cancer: your reputation is important and you are sensitive to others' opinions.

Leo: you are a natural leader and are likely to gain recognition and respect.

Virgo: you are organized and detailed in your methods of reaching your goals.

Libra: you are ethical and charming, and are likely to reach prominence through partnership.

Scorpio: status and renown are gained through your transformative qualities.

Sagittarius: you are visionary and dedicated to guiding others.

Capricorn: you are competitive and ambitious, and are eager for success.

Aquarius: You are prominent in groups and attract like-minded individuals.

Pisces: you are elusive and are attracted to mystery and discovering secrets.

> Look at the sign on your tenth house and its triplicity and quadruplicity, and consider how you express the characteristics and qualities of that sign in the pursuit of your goals and career. Which qualities are you using at the moment? Are any characteristics recognized but latent? How can you develop these?

The position of the ruling planet of the tenth house and any planets situated in this house indicate your needs and desires in the areas of goals, career and prominence, and reveal how you express these. These are the channels through which you pour the energy to decipher and aim for your goals. For instance, Venus in the tenth house indicates that you need to express yourself harmoniously and creatively. One of your goals, to create beauty, and your charming manners and natural friendliness help you to accomplish your aims. You nurture good relationships with colleagues, bosses and others connected with your career or work environment. As you are quietly ambitious, it is likely that your chosen romantic partner will be someone who is successful in their own right.

Planets in the tenth house and career possibilities

Sun: dignified, confident, authoritarian and powerful. Fame is likely. *Ideal careers*: creative arts, design, government, administration.

Moon: attentive, ambitious and success comes through your need to prove yourself. *Ideal careers*: land, real estate, sailing, cooking, caring professions.

Mercury: focused, opinionated, planning power, success through communication. *Ideal careers*: communications, contractors, teaching, computers, information technology.

Venus: upwardly mobile, charming, collaborative, creative/artistic success. *Ideal careers*: arts, design, acting, beauty industry.

Mars: driven, goal-oriented, a leader, status through single-mindedness. *Ideal careers*: sports, military, medicine, manufacturing.

Jupiter: dedication, enthusiasm, focus, recognition and possibly celebrity. *Ideal careers*: religion, philosophy, teaching, business, scientist.

Saturn: ambitious, determined, persevering, workaholic tendencies. *Ideal careers*: business, medicine, mathematics, sciences, politics, craftsperson.

Uranus: unusual career, unconventional, ambitious, success through innovation. *Ideal careers*: astrologer, computing, technology, entrepreneur.

Neptune: creative, visionary, intuitive, success through ability to connect with others. *Ideal careers*: arts, film industry, photography, social work, maritime work.

Pluto: determined, indefatigable, perceptive, success through transformation. *Ideal careers*: Investigation, psychology, medicine, sciences, undercover work.

Chiron: strong willpower, persistent, altruistic, success through healing facility. *Ideal careers*: healing, medicine, sports, teaching, mentoring.

The natural rulers of the tenth house are Capricorn and Saturn. Their influence is slow and steady, determined, willing to plod on and deal with any obstacles that arise. Capricorn, the mountain goat, steps nimbly up steep slopes, confidently placing its hooves in places that are considered to be inaccessible by other less hardy creatures. This astrological sign is patient, persistent and ambitious, with a steady determination and a practical nature. Capricorn is astute, not easily fooled or swayed from the path and is a hard taskmaster with high expectations.

Saturn, its ruling planet, is named after the Roman god Saturn who, in turn, arose from the Greek Cronus, the dour father of the pantheon of Olympian deities, driven to infanticide through his fear of being overthrown by his heirs. Saturn is no pushover. Serious, disciplined and the stern father of the zodiac, his influence gives you the strong push to succeed in whatever you strive for and also the slap on the wrists if you fail to honour his tests of fortitude, self-discipline, adherence to structure and hard work. The position of Saturn in your chart reveals where your expectations are high, and if these expectations are not met, melancholia, depression and introversion tend to occur. Saturn often has a bad press in astrology, yet without these qualities of self-discipline, structure and form, and sheer determination, the ideas may be good but may not be carried through effectively.

Insight

Any planets in the tenth house, and aspects to these, especially if they are also in conjunction to the Midheaven, indicate how you set out and follow your goals. Any likelihood of public recognition, fame, celebrity or notoriety can be seen in tenth house planets and aspects.

Look at the planets in your tenth house and any aspects to these. This gives you strong indications of how and where you direct your energy into your career and the fulfilment of your goals. Write some keywords for any planets situated here and consider what these tell you about your aptitudes and career possibilities.

Insight

The tenth-house sign, and any planets and aspects, can help you to determine which choice of career is best for you. Mercury indicates a career in communication, whether this is through writing, public speaking or technology. Venus indicates a career centred around the areas of art and beauty.

Improving your chances of attainment and success

The careers outlined in the section above on the planets are only a rough guide but can help you to think about how you can use your special talents. Use these as a guideline and consider how any of these fit in with your particular interests. Consider what you feel passionate about, as this can help you to keep your focus and be willing to work towards long-range goals or to undertake further training. Look at other areas of your chart. The second house (earning power) and the sixth house (work, health and service) provide further information that could be useful in strengthening your career path. If you are unsure about whether you are on the best career path for you, this can help you to clarify matters. If your decision feels firm, these houses can give indications of resources on which you can draw.

> Make a list of what you consider to be your strengths and weaknesses regarding your vocation and career. How can you further develop your strengths and work with strengthening any weaknesses? Look at any talents that could be used in your career. These could be practical skills or social skills such as communication and networking.

Insight

You can explore your potential for success by looking at the career and goal-oriented possibilities within the tenth house, and also by exploring the sixth-house influence of work. As the position of Capricorn shows how you use your powers of determination, you can also consider this.

JEN'S CHART

Look back at Jen's chart on page 17. Jen's tenth house is situated in Pisces, which is a mutable water sign. She needs to be able to use her artistic and creative talents, and her visionary, intuitive faculties in her career. Pisces rules the emotions, dreams, visions and the mystical, nebulous side of the personality, which is compelled to go with the flow and to relate through the impact of emotions. Jen's choice of a film-making career is perfect for her because through this she can blend all of her creative talents together. As Pisces is also concerned with experiencing a deep, meaningful connection with others, Jen can fully express her qualities of caring and compassion and her desire to make a difference to the way others think and perceive. Film can be an influential medium, especially when it carries an underlying message, as it is accessible to the masses and is easily absorbed into public consciousness.

The rulers of Pisces are Jupiter and Neptune. Jupiter in Sagittarius in Jen's sixth house reveals that Jen places great emphasis on work that is meaningful to her and that provides a service to others. Her work is her main area of expansion and she has a desire to pass on the knowledge and information that has proved to be useful to her. It is important that Jen's work fulfils her spiritual and philosophical needs, and she is dedicated and enthusiastic. This helps to bring support from those in a position to further her career, as her optimism and energy make potential colleagues and backers feel confident that she can carry through her plans.

Jupiter trine Jen's Moon shows that Jen has an expansive, creative imagination. She is able to access her deep emotions and to use these in order to enhance her creativity and inspire those around her. Close relationships within the family are characteristic of this aspect and Jen is likely to pursue at least some of her career from her home, which acts as a base and foundation.

As Jupiter is in opposition to Venus, this indicates that Jen has a great deal of creative and artistic talent, and a desire to increase her resources and use these fully. Over-spending could cause difficulties, but Jen's visionary qualities help her to overcome setbacks. In the realm of film-making, Jen's Venus position in her chart is important. Jen has Venus in Cancer, in the twelfth house. She has a shy, immensely sensitive side to her nature and prefers to retain an element of privacy regarding her personal life. Her work behind the scenes in the film world is suited to this because she can connect emotionally with her work and aims to use that emotional connection in order to create a message that others can access at an intuitive level. Her desire for harmony, balance and beauty enable her to structure her vision so that it carries an emotional resonance.

Jupiter is trine Mars in the third house. This indicates that Jen is a dynamic, motivational communicator, who is full of ideas and plans that she is enthusiastic about putting into practice. Jen enjoys being where the action is and sets a great deal of that action in motion herself. She is able to confront problems and use the sheer force of her will to find solutions to these.

A square between Jupiter and Pluto can highlight strong-mindedness and a clash of wills. Jen has firm beliefs and is unwilling to compromise, which may be a cause of conflict in her work. She can work with this through being willing to listen to the opinions of others and to discuss her reasons for disagreeing so that matters are clear and no animosity results.

Jupiter opposition the Ascendant indicates that Jen exudes confidence and goodwill towards others. She can gain a great deal in her career through partnerships with others but needs to know that she can keep a degree of independence. Jen finds it hard to hand over her ideas unless she can feel that she will retain an element of control concerning how these will be used. This aspect shows that Jen is able to promote herself through her connections and make them work well for her in her career.

Jupiter sextile MC is very good news for Jen's career. This indicates high standing and professional success, with good fortune coming through the co-operation and high regard of those in power. Jen's cheerfulness, confidence and optimism are a great help to her progress and she is adept at promoting herself and her work. This aspect can also mean that marriage or partnership will be with someone in a position of success and power, and will be emotionally and professionally valuable to her.

Neptune, like Jupiter, is also in Sagittarius in the sixth house. Jen's work must utilize her creative, artistic and visionary faculties, and must foster emotional connections with others in order for her to feel fulfilled. She is very intuitive and actively pours her vision, hopes and dreams into her work. Jen is highly imaginative and the image-making faculty of her mind is strongly developed. This contributes greatly to her choice of career. Jen is idealistic and the Sagittarian influence makes her keen to widely disseminate her creative works so that others can learn from these and make use of them.

Neptune sextile Pluto in the fourth house indicates that Jen seeks to transform others through her vision of fulfilled potential and universal love. This is the foundation of her hopes and dreams for her career. Neptune square MC reveals that Jen's career involves insecurity and unreliability and that, because of her trusting nature, she may be vulnerable to deceit or deception. Fortunately this aspect is tempered by the other strong aspects in Jen's chart which enable her to bounce back after disappointments and to gain the respect and support of those who are in a position to help further her career.

Capricorn is on Jen's seventh house. This indicates that Jen takes partnerships seriously and that there is a likelihood of detailed contracts involved in Jen's career. Capricorn has a strong work ethic and a long-term view, which helps Jen to maintain her vision and focus. Partnership or marriage with someone older than her is very likely.

Saturn in the twelfth house shows that much of Jen's work takes place behind the scenes and involves large organizations that are based strongly on financial acumen and accumulation. If Jen's Saturn had challenging aspects this could hold back her career progress, but fortunately her Saturn aspects are very positive. A trine to Uranus in Libra in the fifth house reveals that Jen is inspired and innovative, but is also disciplined about her creativity and ensures that she takes a practical approach to developing and using her gifts. The sextile to Chiron in Aries in the eleventh house indicates that Jen's aims are to actively use her work in order to help and instruct others.

Keywords for Jen's goals and career: artistic, creative, visionary, image-making faculties, expansion, intuition, support from high places, confidence, optimism, recognition, idealism, emotion, practicality, helpfulness.

GOALS AND CAREER SUMMARY:

▶ *the astrological sign on the tenth house*
▶ *its triplicity and quadruplicity*
▶ *its ruling planet(s)*
▶ *planets in the tenth house*
▶ *aspects to planets in the tenth house*
▶ *the position of Capricorn*
▶ *the position of Saturn.*

10 THINGS TO REMEMBER

1 *Your aims, goals and ambitions are revealed through your tenth house.*

2 *The tenth house is ruled by Capricorn and Saturn.*

3 *The tenth house can indicate your public persona, and possibilities of fame or notoriety.*

4 *The astrological sign on your tenth house shows the area in which your goals and aims are focused.*

5 *Planets in the tenth house reveal the qualities which help you to achieve your goals.*

6 *Planets in aspect to the Midheaven emphasize your goals and strongly impact on your career.*

7 *The ruling planet of the sign on your tenth house shows your needs and desires regarding your goals and career issues.*

8 *The position of Saturn in your chart reveals where you are best able to exercise self-discipline and determination.*

9 *The position of Capricorn in your chart reveals the area in which you have much staying-power and endurance.*

10 *Planets in the tenth house, and aspects to these, give indications of the careers that you may be best suited to.*

16

Social success and group endeavours

In this chapter you will learn:
- *about your friendships and interests*
- *about your approach to group situations*
- *about how you can increase your social success.*

Our earliest ancestors were tribal peoples because the survival of the group and the human race was dependent on each member of the tribe fulfilling their allotted roles and tasks. These small groups gradually merged to create larger tribes and then nations and cultures, and the use of technology has now enabled us to view our world as a global village with instant communication across great distances. This ease of contact only emphasizes how we are still attuned to the need to feel connected to others and to gain a perception of our place in the world through our social, recreational and professional interactions with others.

For an understanding of your social skills and how you interact within groups, the eleventh house is the area to explore. Here you can find out how you interact with others in group situations and discover the common interests that help to forge bonds and a feeling that you are connected with like minds or kindred spirits. How you make friends, the type of friends whom you are drawn to, organizations, clubs or causes that are significant in your life, your persona and role within groups of people, your self-expression and your pursuit of goals that include others are all included in the eleventh house. The groups concerned may be recreational, through which you pursue a hobby or interest. Or they can be connected with an idea, an ideal or a humanitarian cause. Planets within the eleventh house reveal where your loyalties are placed and how you follow these through, and they show how you experience and express a sense of responsibility that encompasses a wider range than your family and close friends.

Challenging aspects with eleventh-house planets can indicate extreme shyness or inability to make friends easily. There may be a sense of isolation or a feeling that somehow you 'don't belong', or conflict within a group, which affects you deeply. Positive aspects concerning the eleventh house indicate mutually beneficial interactions with others, a sense of community within the group or groups of your choice and a feeling of mutual trust, loyalty and the satisfying pursuit of a common goal.

Insight

Your ability to make and sustain friendships, the people you choose to spend your time with, and the types of groups or organizations that you feel an affinity for can all be understood through your eleventh-house placements.

The signs on the eleventh house

Aries: you are dynamic in groups and friendships, a natural leader and need change and stimulation.

Taurus: you are upwardly mobile in groups and enjoy sharing artistic pleasures and pursuits with friends.

Gemini: you are sociable, gregarious, interactive and have a wide circle of friends and interests.

Cancer: the home is your favoured social base. Somewhat retiring, you espouse organizations that help others.

Leo: you take pride in your friends and seek their approbation. In groups you tend to be the leader.

Virgo: you prefer a small group of trusted friends and are active behind the scenes in espousing causes.

Libra: you are cultured, highly sociable and popular, and treasure your friends. Groups connected with the arts and justice appeal to you.

Scorpio: you are private and have small groups of trusted friends, often in high places. There may be sudden transformations in associations.

Sagittarius: you are gregarious and social, and although somewhat aloof you attract many friends. A cause is important to you.

Capricorn: you are reserved and reluctant to involve yourself in groups, but you become more sociable as you grow older.

Aquarius: intellectuals, rebels and innovators attract you. You may be involved in humanitarian organizations or causes.

Pisces: you are generous, caring and idealistic, but you feel easily betrayed. Friendships and groups provide a sense of belonging.

Look at the astrological sign on your eleventh house and its triplicity and quadruplicity. How do you express these characteristics and qualities through your friendships and group activities? What does this tell you about how you use your social skills?

Insight

The sign on your eleventh house indicates your approach to friendships and groups. Gemini shows a wide range of friends, interests and group activities. Capricorn indicates that you take time to open up to others, and are cautious about your involvements until you feel able to commit yourself.

The ruling planet(s) of the sign on your eleventh house and any planets and their aspects that are situated in this house indicate how you express and follow through on your needs and desires for social interaction that is meaningful to you. This interaction is not superficial but is geared towards how you seek to belong in some way and how you seek to feel that you are joining with others as a means of exploring your sense of purpose. The eleventh house deals with your concerns with others and with the wider world, as well as your friendships and social activities.

For instance, Mercury in the eleventh house reveals that communication is vastly important to you. You like to be surrounded by people and spend a great deal of time interacting face to face, on the phone and through the internet. Ideas fascinate you and you have an unusual, original, perceptive and fertile mind. You are drawn to characters who share your passion for communication and you are interested in concepts that can lead the way, especially when these are technological or scientific. You are everyone's friend and have a wide and diverse range of friends and acquaintances, but you dislike being hampered or tied down, so find it hard to allow yourself to get too close to people. There is likely to be much coming and going, with some connections fading out and new ones taking their place. You need to feel stimulated and interested by the people around you. Social issues and humanitarian principles and groups gain your support easily and you invest a great deal of energy into any causes that you support.

Planets in the eleventh house, sociability and groups

Sun: sociable, group-minded, communicative, observant, a natural leader.

Moon: many interests, networking, groups as extended family, friendly, caring.

Mercury: diverse, communicative, perceptive, humanitarian, enquiring mind.

Venus: friendly, social, creative, partner could be met through group activities, unconventional.

Mars: reforming, independent, outgoing, pro-active, inventive.

Jupiter: expansive, humanitarian, optimistic, co-operative, curious, principled.

Saturn: loyal, fair, practical, prominence within group or organization.

Uranus: charismatic, individual, magnetic, innovative ideas, unconventional.

Neptune: idealistic, kind, drawn to causes, humanitarian, creative/ artistic groups.

Pluto: revolutionary, transformative, ethical, insightful, desire to be in control.

Chiron: compassionate, explorative, progressive friends or groups, self-help.

Insight

Any planets situated in your eleventh house show how you interact in your social dealings. Because this house also governs humanitarian principles, planets which are placed here can reveal issues which you feel concern about, and commitment to, and show how you express this.

The natural rulers of the eleventh house are Aquarius and Uranus. Their influence is innovative, curious and enquiring, with an urge to be involved with others in order to explore ideas and break new ground that will be of use to the human race. Aquarius is the lateral thinker of the zodiac – the innovator who desires to rebel against outworn ideas and concepts and bring a new and unique vision that will benefit humanity as a whole. Open-minded, innovative, stimulating and friendly to all in a cool, detached way, sociable and free-thinking, the Aquarian mind acts through flashes of inspiration and insight that provide an alternative viewpoint. Understanding and facilitating the power of the group mind to create lasting changes is the focus of Aquarius. The area of your chart in which Aquarius is found can reveal where you feel a need to rebel against the status quo and where you tend to gather with like-minded people with a common aim or cause.

Uranus is the planet of change, and its position in your chart shows where you will seek out new pathways to understanding and use your powers of perception and insight to their fullest. It indicates the types of friendships and groups that are most appealing to you and through which you can assert your individuality and find openings for your desire to discover something fresh and new. Uranus is the inventor of the zodiac and in your chart it can reveal a fascination with metaphysics, technology and the sciences. Its position in your chart shows where you are always looking for a way in which to practically apply knowledge, or perhaps you have a unique slant on the world that can be inspirational to those around you.

Look at the planets in your eleventh house and any aspects to these. How can you develop the characteristics and qualities of these planets and channel them into fostering ideas, friendships and group activities? Write down some keywords for these planets and think about how you are currently using their qualities in your life.

Insight

Aspects to eleventh-house planets add to your insight into how you engage with other people in a group setting. Depending on the planets and aspects involved, challenging aspects can indicate traits such as shyness or argumentativeness, while easy aspects indicate that you are socially fluent.

Increasing your social success and group activities

Your eleventh house, the planets within it and the position of Aquarius and Uranus in your chart give you a great deal of information about how you relate to others in a social and group setting. In order to increase your opportunities for furthering your success in this area, it is important, first of all, to understand what your needs are and how you respond to them. If you are innately shy and prefer to avoid large gatherings of people, you will be more comfortable about involvement within small groups, where you feel secure. This will help you to gain confidence and enable you to cope better with larger groups when these are necessary. By looking at the potentials in your chart, you can decide which of these holds the most interest for you and take steps to actively develop these. If you are sociable and outgoing, your chart can give indications of how to channel your interests most effectively.

It is helpful to look at your third house, which reveals communication skills, and your fifth house, which shows the areas in which you shine, as these contribute to the development and expression of your social skills.

Make a list of what you perceive to be your social strengths and weaknesses. Consider how you can develop and further utilize your strengths. Now look at how you can turn your weaknesses into more helpful attributes. Do you need to stand out in a crowd? Do you prefer to feel part of a large group that helps you to explore your interests? Or are you happiest with just a few trusted friends? By finding your comfort zone, you can gain the confidence to move beyond it into new areas of discovery.

Insight

You can further enhance your social skills through exploring the components of the third house of communication and the fifth house of recreation. Looking at the positions of Aquarius and the planet Mercury helps with understanding of how you communicate within a social or group environment.

JEN'S CHART

Look back at Jen's chart on page 17. Jen's eleventh house begins in Aries, which is a cardinal fire sign. This house, with Jen's opposite fifth house, takes up a great deal of space in the two-dimensional view of her chart, indicating that Jen's friendships, social connections and group activities are of major significance in her life. Jen is active and dynamic in her social dealings, likes to be in the forefront of what is going on and has natural leadership abilities. She pours a great deal of energy into her social dealings and friendships, and is viewed as being a motivational force who inspires others. Jen is clearly an 'ideas' person and enjoys the company of others. Groups and friendships that enable her to express her creative side are appealing to her and she is drawn to those who are considered to be leaders in their field and who provide the stimulation that she enjoys.

As the eleventh house also encompasses much of Taurus, Jen is practical and determined. She is able to further her ambitions through connecting with kindred spirits who are in a position to assist her and mentor her.

The ruler of Aries is Mars, which is in Leo in the third house. Dynamic, stimulating conversation and the exchange of ideas form the cornerstone of Jen's social life. She enjoys discussions that make her think and which spark off more ideas and possibilities. Jen is a mental explorer and is keen to discover and map new terrain in the realms of ideas, and to decipher how these can be usefully employed.

As Mars is trine Jupiter, Jen is courageous and is willing to lay herself on the line in the pursuit of her aims. She 'thinks big' and is good at taking the initiative in her relationships with those around her. Optimistic, energetic and forward-thinking, Jen is drawn to groups as a means of improving the lives of others in some way. She has a strong sense of adventure and is always willing to pitch in with group aims and needs, and to give her all for what she believes in. Mars square Neptune in Sagittarius in the sixth house indicates that Jen's enthusiasm about her ideas and impulses can lead her to be taken advantage of in a work situation that is associated with her friendships and group endeavours. Mars trine Chiron in the eleventh house reveals that Jen is altruistic and desires to use her understanding and experiences to help others. She may take on a mentoring role with friends or within group activities. Mars in opposition to the MC indicates that Jen's home life and early years were formative in developing her strong character and brings about a desire to get her own way and to win through over any obstacles.

The presence of Taurus, which forms half of Jen's eleventh house, indicates that Jen's Venus, which is in Cancer in her twelfth house, is also a powerful influence on her friendships and group associations. Venus is conjunct Jen's Ascendant, showing that she is charming and caring, and that people are easily attracted to her. She may experience conflict between her dynamic Mars side, which desires to be in the thick of all that is going on, and her rather shy emotional side, which genuinely likes people and wants to be liked but needs time alone in order to tap into her artistic and creative side. With these two conflicting influences it is likely that Jen is confident and outspoken with those whom she knows and trusts, but takes her time in getting to know new people and is more comfortable if they approach her first of all. Once secure, she is happy to take the initiative and is proactive in developing friendships.

Jen's Venus in opposition to Jupiter in Sagittarius in the sixth house and square Pluto in Libra in the fourth house indicates that Jen easily feels insecure and needs assurance that she is valued and cared for. This underlying insecurity leads Jen to feel a need to be in control and she is capable of masking this through being forceful or through using the emotions as a tool to getting her own way when other strategies do not appear to be working. As Venus is trine the MC, Jen expresses her urge towards harmony and her creative and artistic impulses through her career and is met with friendships, co-operation and support from others, which helps to further her goals. Her group activities and friendships are closely affiliated to her passions, which are fully expressed through the medium of her career, and she is likely to be involved in film-making groups and have many friends in that field.

Chiron in Aries in the eleventh house reveals that Jen needs to express her altruistic impulses through friendships and group activities. She has a deep desire to help others and to pass on the knowledge and understanding that she has gained through application, study, deduction and sheer hard work. Chiron reveals the area in which inner wounds are explored and where steps are taken in order to bring about a degree of healing. In the eleventh house this can indicate that health issues may have emotional roots and are closely connected to experiences involving a breakdown of trust. Chiron is trine Jen's Sun, Mercury and Mars in Leo in the third house, showing that Jen has immense powers of resilience and can heal old wounds through her optimism and inner self-belief. She is likely to use her experiences in order to help others, and is able to communicate in a powerful manner. With her innate mentoring skills, Jen uses her Chiron–Sun–Mercury–Mars trines to actively be of use, as is apparent in the support and information website for film-makers that she has set up. A sextile between Chiron and Saturn indicates that Jen is able to structure her time in order to create space for the various categorizations of friendships and group involvements. Through this, she is able to accomplish a great deal as her orderly mind helps her to see clearly and to prioritize.

Aquarius, the ruler of the eleventh house, is situated over Jen's eighth and ninth houses. She is committed to her friendships and group activities, and views these as a means of inner discovery and of broadening knowledge and disseminating ideas. Jen's Uranus is in Libra in the fifth house, indicating that she needs to express herself creatively and be involved with friendships and groups which connect her with unique individuals and lead to the development of innovative ideas. As Uranus is in opposition to Chiron in Jen's eleventh house, this indicates that she is strongly independent and individual, and desires to use her skills in order to bring benefits to others.

Keywords for Jen's social success and group endeavours: unique, individual, helpful, mentoring skills, friendly, committed, altruistic, charming, communicative, dynamic, enthusiastic, needs some time alone.

SOCIAL SUCCESS AND GROUP ENDEAVOURS SUMMARY:

▶ *the astrological sign on the eleventh house*
▶ *triplicity and quadruplicity*
▶ *its ruling planet(s)*
▶ *planets in the eleventh house*
▶ *aspects to planets in the eleventh house*
▶ *the position of Aquarius*
▶ *the position of Uranus.*

10 THINGS TO REMEMBER

1 Your social skills and interests, and the type of people and organizations that you are drawn to, are indicated in the eleventh house.

2 The eleventh house is ruled by Aquarius, Uranus and Saturn.

3 How you interact with others in your social sphere can be explored through the eleventh house.

4 The eleventh house rules groups and organizations, both recreational and humanitarian.

5 The astrological sign on your eleventh house indicates how you respond to social and group situations.

6 Planets in the eleventh house reveal how you interact with others beyond your immediate circle.

7 Aspects to eleventh-house planets indicate gifts and challenges concerning your social skills.

8 You can increase your social skills through exploring both the third house and eleventh house.

9 The position of Aquarius in your chart shows in which area you are committed to group activities or common goals.

10 The position of Uranus in your chart reveals the area in which you express innovation and share new ideas.

17

Your inner life

In this chapter you will learn:
- *about the private inner you*
- *about your secret dreams and fantasies*
- *about how to understand messages from your subconscious mind.*

What are your inner hopes and dreams? What characterizes your hidden, private self? Which elements of your subconscious mind have the most subtle but pervasive effects on your personality?

During our waking lives we are subjected to a vast range of impressions, thoughts, feelings and experiences; far too many for our conscious minds to interpret, and to attempt to do so with every impression would be too much for sane comprehension. Some of these impressions consist of information that is necessary at this moment, and the conscious mind swiftly analyses and categorizes these so that we can make decisions and form judgements. Others are too subtle or chaotic to be useful to the conscious mind and these are relegated to the subconscious mind, where they lie quietly until some word, action or association stirs the depths and brings them to the surface.

The subconscious mind is the mysterious area of the psyche that holds the sum of our past experiences and acts as a storehouse for memories, feelings and impressions. Reflexive thoughts and actions and conditioned responses are a product of the workings of the subconscious mind. The currency of the subconscious mind is symbols which we interpret through associations that have meaning for us. Dreams reflect experiences we have not been able to integrate, or bring messages of our hopes or fears. Inner feelings and promptings tell us when to be wary or when to take a leap of faith, and instinctive or intuitive preferences or repulsions guide us towards or away from certain situations or people.

Ultimately the purpose of the subconscious mind is to protect us, but sometimes, through misinterpreting its messages, it can trap us and hold back our growth. Addictions, obsessions, compulsions, illusions and delusions are products of the shadow element of the subconscious mind. The gifts of the subconscious mind are dreams, fantasies, intuition and the creative and artistic faculties. Some of the greatest artists and scientists have developed their brilliance through learning to understand how the conscious, subconscious and unconscious aspects of the mind work: Einstein, whose daydream of riding on a beam of light led to his theory of relativity; Kekule, whose dream of a snake swallowing its own tail led to the discovery of the structure of benzene; artists such as Dali and Picasso, whose work tapped into the surreal landscape of the subconscious. The list goes on and on.

The area of your birth chart that gives information about your subconscious mind is the twelfth house. Here you can discover what is occurring behind the scenes and discover the form that your secrets, dreams and fantasies take. Your approach towards, and feelings about, mysticism and spirituality are revealed here. Predisposition to illusions and delusions, the likelihood of seclusion, incarceration or involvement with institutions, the presence of hidden enemies and any escapist tendencies are indicated in this house. Here, you can also discover the nature of your inner self, the source of intuition, inspiration, visionary gifts, trust and the qualities of compassion. The twelfth house carries associations with universal truths and experiences through its link with what Jung called the superconscious – the transcendental sense of interconnection with the spiritual source.

The subconscious mind, which you can find information on in the twelfth house, is a storehouse for all of your accumulated memories and impressions. Much of this information is hidden from conscious reasoning, but can rise to the surface when an image, dream or memory acts as a trigger.

The astrological sign on your twelfth house and its triplicity and quadruplicity reveal the qualities through which you access your subconscious, unconscious and superconscious mind. Whereas your Sun sign reveals your essential nature, the first house shows your outer personality, and the seventh house indicates your relationships, the twelfth house describes the secret 'inner you'. If planets situated in your twelfth house are well-aspected, this shows that you have a healthy link with the subtle areas of your mind and experience this through compassion and empathy towards others, through well-developed intuition and through being able to interpret the symbols of the subconscious mind and enhance your creativity and sense of connection with others. Challenging aspects can reveal naivety, susceptibility to manipulation, illusions or delusions and the possibility of addiction or psychological imbalance.

As an example, Scorpio on the twelfth house would indicate that you are deep, secretive and introverted, with a powerful need and desire to delve beneath the surface and to understand the subtle workings of the mind. Your dream-life would be filled with messages, some of which could even prove to be prophetic, and you would intuitively understand the symbolism within these. With positive aspects, you would be an observer of human nature, perceptive and intuitive, and would channel your drives into investigatory or exploratory work. Nothing would escape your penetrating gaze and your understanding could lead to personal transformation which would strongly influence others. If there are challenging aspects, this could lead to an over-ruling temptation to control and manipulate the minds of others because you would understand the triggers that set off conditioned responses.

An obsessive, addictive psychological element could manifest through sex, alcohol, drugs or through power-seeking.

The signs on the twelfth house

Aries: you appear outwardly calm but inwardly you are courageous and assertive.

Taurus: family secrets influence you and you worry subconsciously about security.

Gemini: you need time alone to develop your ideas and tend to verbalize emotional upsets.

Cancer: you are sensitive and easily hurt but find it hard to express your feelings.

Leo: your inner strength belies your outward calm and you have secret reserves of willpower.

Virgo: you are prone to worry but are able to organize and discriminate.

Libra: you are charming and fair-minded but may secretly over-spend.

Scorpio: you are secretive, with investigative abilities, but wish for control.

Sagittarius: outwardly you are businesslike but inwardly very spiritually-oriented.

Capricorn: you are honest and trustworthy, but fearful. Organization is your source of strength.

Aquarius: you are humanitarian and compassionate but need a great deal of support.

Pisces: you are empathetic and caring yet easily tend to feel isolated and alone.

Insight

The astrological sign on your twelfth house is the gateway to understanding the workings of your subconscious mind. Your unconscious responses and reactions to external triggers are based on the qualities of the sign on your twelfth house.

Look at the sign on your twelfth house, its triplicity and quadruplicity, and consider what this tells you about your inner nature. How do you express these qualities? Do you immediately recognize these or are some deeply hidden from your conscious awareness?

Planets in the twelfth house and your inner life

Sun: mystical, dreamy, shy, sensitive, introverted, compassionate, artistic.

Moon: sensitive, psychic, introverted, vulnerable, emotional, intuitive, gentle.

Mercury: memories, unconscious mental patterns, shy, intuitive, visionary, secretive.

Venus: sensitive, dreamy, idealistic, sympathetic, imaginative, visionary, artistic.

Mars: non-confrontational, creatively pro-active, secretive, spiritual impetus.

Jupiter: idealistic, altruistic, generous, sympathetic, introspective, caring.

Saturn: creative, practical, structured, intuitive, loneliness, insights into mind.

Uranus: perceptive, sensitive, empathetic, deeply intuitive, humanitarian.

Neptune: visionary, mystical, artistic gifts, reclusive, empathetic, emotional.

Pluto: secretive, introverted, attuned to subconscious, perceptive, inner purpose.

Chiron: significant dreams, introspective, compassionate, lonely, desire to heal.

Insight

Planets in the twelfth house reveal how you experience your deepest, most hidden thoughts and feelings. Challenging aspects can result in issues involving gullibility, naivety or obsessions, whereas easy aspects can indicate intuition, compassion and spiritual attunement.

The natural rulers of the twelfth house are Pisces, Neptune and Jupiter. Their influences are mystical, intuitive and spiritually expansive. Pisces, symbolized by two fish swimming in opposite directions, is the sign of the compassionate dreamer, the shy idealist with a desire to take care of the world. Easily moved by others, subject to emotional upheaval because the boundaries between the self and others are permeable, and with a tendency to shift swiftly between moods, this is the sign of the mystic and artist. The Piscean nature is secretive, easily hurt and offended but longs to be of use to those who are in need. The idealism of this sign makes Pisces prone to woolgathering and fantasies and there is a susceptibility to disappointment, betrayal and disillusionment when these ideals are not met.

Neptune governs emotional sensitivity and the image-making faculties of the mind. Visualization, meditation and all forms of art are ruled by this planet and a strong Neptune can indicate tremendous creative gifts within the expressive and visual arts. Drawn towards the intangible and nebulous, Neptune can reveal insight into dreams and your spiritual nature and a deep compassion for humanity, but its shadow side is fantasy, escapism, illusion and delusion.

Jupiter's expansive influence is experienced through its rulership of Pisces as a search for deep spiritual meaning. Benevolent and optimistic, this planet adds impetus to the trusting element of the Piscean nature through the belief that all will turn out as it should. The philosophical qualities of Jupiter are channelled into a quest for inner meaning when attuned to its Piscean ruler and emphasizes the growth process that results through making the most of potential.

Look at the planets in the twelfth house and any aspects that are made to these. Their characteristics and qualities reveal how you experience and express your inner nature and can inform you about your intuition, dreams, fantasies, artistic and creative impulses, and your spiritual path and development. Write down some keywords for these, and consider what messages they hold for you.

Insight

Through looking at the sign on the twelfth house, its triplicity and quadruplicity, planets positioned there and aspects to these, you can discover much about how and why you instinctively act and react.

Strengthening your connection with the inner you

Your exploration of the twelfth house will have provided information about your inner life and how your subconscious mind influences your attitudes, actions, reactions and impulses. Through investigating this, you can gain insight into how and why you set up particular patterns in your modes of thinking and self-expression. Consider which of these are useful to you and which ones are the result of past experiences that are now defunct. This insight into the previously hidden workings of your mind can be revelatory and can spur you on to realize your potential. You can further strengthen this connection by setting aside brief periods of time alone in which to contemplate or meditate. This helps you to forge a deep and lasting channel between the inner you and your conscious mind because this influential part of yourself is revealed through moments of quiet reflection. Understanding the causes can enable you to see their effects and to feel more empowered and in control of your life.

> List the qualities that you regard as being your strengths and weaknesses. Do any of these qualities surprise you? Think carefully about these for a few minutes. How can you use the qualities of your inner self in a conscious way for self-understanding and self-empowerment? Which of these can you choose to purposefully develop?

Insight

Your intuitive abilities can be enhanced through looking into what your twelfth house tells you about your inner self. Delving into this allows your subconscious mind to reveal some of its secrets and, as you focus on the 'inner you', the qualities of insight and intuition naturally expand and develop.

JEN'S CHART

Look back at Jen's chart on page 17. Jen's twelfth house begins with Taurus, a fixed earth sign, and encompasses all of Gemini, a mutable air sign. Jen's inner nature is closely bound to all forms of communication, which she needs to apply in practical ways. There is an introverted element to Jen's nature and she needs time on her own so that she can formulate, contemplate and develop the ideas which she then puts into operation. Jen keeps her inner thoughts and ideas to herself and is reluctant to share these until she feels that she has formulated them coherently and laid foundations for their application – only then will she share them with others. She derives a subtle pleasure through this secretiveness and may give out hints or clues and enjoy deflecting questions. However, she gives nothing away until she feels that she is ready to do so.

Jen seeks to find new ways of looking at the world and it is important to her that other people benefit through the ideas and plans that she puts in motion. She is articulate when she feels confident but has a shy, withdrawn side, which takes over in unfamiliar surroundings or with new friends and acquaintances. Her dreams are likely to be vivid and to give her insights into how she can live her life or accomplish her plans. Jen has a strong mystical side and finds this a fascinating area of exploration and discovery.

The ruling planet of Taurus is Venus and the ruling planet of Gemini is Mercury. Jen's Venus is situated in Cancer in her twelfth house so gives further insight into Jen's inner self. She is extremely sensitive to the thoughts and feelings of others and her intuition is highly developed. Creative, artistic, with the ability to visualize and to see ideas in the form of images, Jen is caring, kind and compassionate but her sensitivity makes her easily hurt. When upset, she withdraws both emotionally and physically, and she needs a retreat where she feels safe and secure. There could be a tendency to wish to mother the world and she is protective of those who are close to her. Jen is closely attuned to her mystical and spiritual nature, and is likely to have moments of experiencing an intense sense of universal connection.

Venus conjunct the Ascendant reveals that Jen naturally draws others to her. She is warm and loving, and her genuine liking of people is a quality that brings her many friends. As Venus is in opposition to Jupiter in Sagittarius in the sixth house, Jen's ability to create images is used a great deal in her work and helps to expand the skills that help her to progress and grow inwardly as well as in the outer world. Her independent streak can mean that she is reluctant to give away control over her creative projects. She has sound business sense and is cautious about leaping forward too fast. There may be a subconscious fear of others using her ideas for their own personal gain. This is further emphasized by Jen's Venus–Pluto square involving the fourth house, and indicates that experiences of being controlled or manipulated may have set up an emotional pattern of instinctive wariness. Jen can use this caution to her advantage as long as she can also be aware of whom she can trust, and listen to her inner promptings. Venus trine the MC shows that Jen's visionary faculties form the foundation for her career and indicates popularity, success and acclaim in her career as a film-maker.

Jen's Mercury is in Leo in the third house and is strongly positively aspected. Jen's communication skills are well honed and her sense of herself as rather shy and introverted is not likely to be noticed by those around her unless she chooses to communicate her inner feelings. She keeps this well hidden. Mercury is sextile Saturn, which is also in the twelfth house in Gemini. Jen has an appreciation of, and talent for, form and structure and works hard to develop this. This is immensely useful in her career as she is methodical, patient and careful to ensure that everything is in the right place. Jen needs to be sure that there is always a practical application for her ideas; woolgathering and fantasy only interest her when they are used in the early stages of opening to the creative process.

Mercury is also sextile Uranus, which is in the fifth house. Jen is a visionary, with ideas that may be perceived as revolutionary by others who are involved in Jen's creative field. She experiences flashes of intuition and insight, which lead to the development of unusual, innovative ideas. Jen is easily inspired and is able to make mental connections between ideas or subjects that do not initially appear to have any relationship between them. Her ability to access her inner life through meditation, contemplation, dreams and symbols has a profound outward effect on her dealings with others.

Mercury trine Chiron in Aries in the eleventh house shows that Jen is finely attuned to the suffering in the world and has a desire to help alleviate this. She has a crusading instinct and may be involved in humanitarian groups and use her work as a forum for this.

Saturn is in Gemini in the twelfth house. This indicates that Jen's shy side can take over when she is hurt or offended and can trigger withdrawal, depression or feelings of isolation. At times, she may feel that others do not understand her. Saturn is considered to be the planet of karma, of cause and effect and, as the twelfth house is also the house of karma, this is a potent, though not always emotionally comfortable, position. Jen enjoys working in the background and does not always expect recognition for her achievements. She has an intuitive understanding of spiritual laws and principles, believes in the principles of reincarnation and is likely to feel that she is an 'old soul' who has experienced a great deal in both past incarnations and in this life.

Saturn trine Uranus in the fifth house, with both of these planets also sextile Mercury, brings an instinctive and intuitive understanding of how and why things work. Jen's humanitarian qualities are highly developed and she uses her ability to grasp form and structure and then communicate this clearly in order to forge connections with others, which bring about sudden and unexpected benefits for all concerned.

Pisces, the natural ruler of Jen's twelfth house, is on Jen's tenth house. This reveals that Jen uses her insights, visionary gifts and creativity as the main tools in her career goals. She dreams big and is likely to use systems such as visualization and cosmic ordering as methods through which to keep focused on her goals.

Jupiter and Neptune are both in Sagittarius in the sixth house, Jen's house of work, health and service. She is consciously aware of a desire to make the world a better place and to use her qualities of inspiration and optimism as part of her plan. With the interpretation of Jen's twelfth house there are indications that Jen has a subconscious desire to bring joy to those around her through her connection with her spiritual source, which she sees as infinitely expansive and abundant. The Neptune–MC square indicates that others may not always share her vision, but her Jupiter–MC sextile shows that she will be successful in using her work as a means of transmitting positive messages, which will be picked up subconsciously by those who see her films.

Keywords for Jen's inner life: shy, retiring, sensitive, easily hurt, inspirational, mystical, spiritual, intuitive, artistic, creative, a practical dreamer, innovator, structure and form, caring, compassionate, idealistic, altruistic.

INNER LIFE SUMMARY:

▶ *the astrological sign on the twelfth house*
▶ *its triplicity and quadruplicity*
▶ *its ruling planet(s)*
▶ *planets in the twelfth house*
▶ *aspects to planets in the twelfth house*
▶ *the position of Pisces*
▶ *the position of Neptune*
▶ *the position of Jupiter.*

10 THINGS TO REMEMBER

1   The twelfth house rules the subconscious mind and the deepest aspects of yourself.

2   The parts of your nature which you keep private, hidden or secret are revealed in your twelfth house.

3   Dreams, buried memories and impressions are governed by the twelfth house.

4   The twelfth house is ruled by Pisces, Neptune and Venus.

5   Planets in the twelfth house reveal how you express your inner self.

6   Positive aspects to twelfth-house planets indicate compassion, altruism and spirituality.

7   Challenging aspects to the twelfth house can indicate traits such as obsessive or addictive behaviour.

8   Through exploring your twelfth house you can gain insight into your deepest patterns and motivations.

9   Your innermost hopes, dreams and fantasies can be found in your twelfth house.

10 Through bringing twelfth-house qualities to consciousness you can overcome blocks and develop inherent gifts.

Part three
Astrology and other systems

18

Numerology

In this chapter you will learn:
- *about what numerology is*
- *about what the numbers symbolize*
- *about combining numerology and astrology.*

As you will have discovered through interpreting your birth chart, astrology can reveal a great deal of information about you and can be of immense use in providing a means to self-understanding and self-empowerment. This ancient art is related to other systems, which include numerology and the tarot. You may wish to explore these and to focus further on your goals through principles such as cosmic ordering as aids to fulfilling your potential. The systems that are outlined in this third section are only described in brief, but if you find any of these interesting there are many good books available which explore them in detail.

Insight

Numerology is an ancient system for understanding the universe we live in. As both the universe and our lives contain patterns, the science of numbers explores how order emerges from what appears to be random and chaotic.

Although numerology has its roots in even earlier times, the father of numerology as we understand it today was Pythagoras, a mathematician and philosopher in Ancient Greece (569–470 BC). He stated that, 'The world is built upon the power of numbers' and considered that the patterns of everything in the cosmos could be understood through the mystical application of their numbers. Since his time, the principles of numerology have been used for character analysis, divination and magic.

> **Insight**
> In both numerology and astrology the date of birth is a vital component for character analysis. In astrology, each sign, house and planet has a number which helps to define the nature of the information given about your personality and how you express yourself.

Numerology and astrology fit well together. As methods of character analysis, the system that is used to create a numerology interpretation corresponds closely with the interpretation of your astrological chart. The date of birth is fundamental to both systems and in numerology your name also provides in-depth information about your character and self-expression. As each number has a symbolic meaning, you can use the numbers as an aid to remembering the basic principles of the astrological signs and of including even more information in the interpretation of your chart. Here is a simple guide to what the numbers reveal.

> **Insight**
> Through understanding the symbolic and esoteric meaning of numbers you can find it easier to remember the information in both astrology and numerology. These two systems each enhance the other.

The astrological signs and numerology

0 *completion, limitlessness, potential, the Divine.*

1 *(Aries): will, initiative, courage, independence, leadership, individuality, beginnings, pioneering, the active impulse to manifest, the conscious mind, active.*

2 *(Taurus): duality, polarity, co-operation, balance, stability, unity, inter-dependence, subconscious, yin/yang, positive/ negative, receptive.*

3 *(Gemini): growth, manifestation, abundance, interaction, communication, the child, self-expression, enthusiasm, creativity, imagination, intellect, completion.*

4 *(Cancer): nurturing, stability, boundaries, foundation, practicality, loyalty, patience, love of the earth.*

5 *(Leo): action, dynamism, individuality, versatility, the microcosm of the macrocosm, curiosity, attraction, creativity, inner child, playfulness.*

6 *(Virgo): involvement, harmony, equilibrium, polarity, balance, reaction, sympathy, understanding, healing, service, perfectionist, humanity.*

7 *(Libra): the mind, thoughts, consciousness, divinity, sacrifice, philosophy, wisdom, harmony, connection.*

8 *(Scorpio): control, power, the 'double four', achievement, success, manifestation, authority, intelligence, rebirth, regeneration.*

9 *(Sagittarius): completion, humanitarianism, generosity, benevolence, healing, mentoring, fulfilment, accomplishment, attainment.*

The double numbers are viewed as having a metaphysical significance, and are harmonics of the numbers that, when single digits are added together, create a single number.

10 *(Capricorn): added together is reduced to 1. Rebirth, authority, completion of a cycle, spiritual law.*

11 *(Aquarius): added together is reduced to 2. Artistic impulses, inspiration, intuition, revelation, visionary gifts, genius.*

12 *(Pisces): added together is reduced to 3. Cosmic order, coming together of material and spiritual, wisdom, compassion, understanding.*

Insight

Each astrological sign follows a sequence. This can also be viewed as a natural progression, from the dynamic, outward-looking number 1 of Aries to the humanitarianism and independence of the number 9 and Sagittarius, and on to the compassion of numbers 12 and 3 of Pisces.

The planets and numerology

Each planet is associated with a number. By looking at the interpretations of the numbers given with the astrological signs, you can gain an extra perspective on their qualities.

Sun: 1	Jupiter: 3
Moon: 2	Saturn: 8
Mercury: 5	Uranus: 9 and 4
Venus: 6	Neptune: 7
Mars: 4	Pluto: 0

Insight

Each planet is allocated a number which further explains its characteristics and qualities. The number 1, represented by the Sun, governs the will, the conscious mind, and leadership qualities. The number 7, symbolized by Neptune, governs wisdom and a deep sense of connection.

10 THINGS TO REMEMBER

1   *Numerology uses the symbolism of numbers for understanding the universe.*

2   *A basic understanding of numerology is useful in astrology and other systems.*

3   *Pythagoras was considered to be the 'father' of numerology.*

4   *A numerology chart reveals similar information to a natal chart.*

5   *As with astrology, the date of birth is important in numerology.*

6   *Every number has a symbolic meaning which has relevance to the personality.*

7   *The number for each astrological sign corresponds with the qualities of that sign.*

8   *The number of each planet helps you to further understand its qualities.*

9   *Double numbers are added together to create a single number.*

10   *When you consider numerological meaning this adds depth to astrological interpretation.*

19

Astrology and the tarot

In this chapter you will learn:
- *about how the modern tarot emerged*
- *about the correspondences with astrology*
- *about combining tarot and astrology.*

> **Insight**
> The tarot is a system of divination and self-understanding
> which explores the diverse elements within the psyche
> through the use of symbolic imagery on a set of 78 illustrated
> cards.

Like astrology, the roots of the tarot dig deep into the ancient
past. There are many theories about the beginnings of the
tarot and its use in Ancient Egypt, but its history as a widely
used set of cards begins in fifteenth-century Milan. Bonifacio
Bembo, an artist, designed a game called Tarocchi for the
Visconti family of Milan, and these cards were used later as
a gambling game and for divination. The Tarocchi consisted
of four suits, each with 14 pip cards and 22 cards called the
trionfi, or trumps, which depicted scenes that were said to
represent the court. Although the trionfi were viewed on a
superficial level as medieval social types, qualities or virtues,
these 22 cards were imbued with esoteric significance and
were considered to have links with a series of archetypes
and with the 22 letters of the Hebrew alphabet.

In the eighteenth century, a French occultist called Antoine Court
de Gebelin asserted that the Tarot, its French name, was a remnant
of the Egyptian Book of Thoth and was intended to transfer
knowledge. In the nineteenth century, Alphonse Louis Constant
(known as Eliphas Levy) linked these cards to the kabbala, which
also carries astrological symbolism, and the tarot became popular
as a tool for self-understanding and divination.

The 78 tarot cards each carry an astrological resonance. The 22
Major Arcana cards (or trumps) are each ruled by an astrological
sign or planet. The 56 Minor Arcana cards are associated with
the triplicities and with the configurations of the planets in
astrological signs. If you are interested in working with the
tarot as well as astrology, it can be useful to consider the cards'
astrological relationships as this enables you to remember
the cards and brings depth to interpretation.

The Major Arcana

0 The Fool: Uranus
I The Magician: Mercury
II The High Priestess: the Moon
III The Empress: Venus

IV The Emperor: Aries
V The Hierophant: Taurus
VI The Lovers: Gemini
VII The Chariot: Cancer
VIII Strength: Leo
IX The Hermit: Virgo
X The Wheel of Fortune: Jupiter
XI Justice: Libra
XII The Hanged Man: Neptune
XIII Death: Scorpio
XIV Temperance: Sagittarius
XV The Devil: Capricorn
XVI The Tower: Mars
XVII The Star: Aquarius
XVIII The Moon: Pisces
XIX The Sun: the Sun
XX Judgement: Pluto
XXI The World: Saturn

Insight

The Major Arcana in the tarot symbolizes archetypal energies which reveal both your inner nature and the life-path which you are engaged in exploring. The astrological signs and planets which rule each card enable you to gain an immediate impression of the qualities of a particular card.

The Minor Arcana

Wands	Cups
Ace: pure fire element	pure water element
2: Mars in Aries	Venus in Cancer
3: the Sun in Aries	Mercury in Cancer
4: Venus in Aries	the Moon in Cancer
5: Saturn in Leo	Mars in Scorpio
6: Jupiter in Leo	the Sun in Scorpio
7: Mars in Leo	Venus in Scorpio
8: Mercury in Sagittarius	Saturn in Pisces
9: the Sun in Sagittarius	Jupiter in Pisces
10: Saturn in Sagittarius	Mars in Pisces
Page: potential of fire signs	potential of water signs
Knight: Sagittarius	Pisces
Queen: Leo	Scorpio
King: Aries	Cancer

Swords	Pentacles
Ace: pure air element	pure earth element
2: the Moon in Libra	Jupiter in Capricorn
3: Saturn in Libra	Mars in Capricorn
4: Jupiter in Libra	the Sun in Capricorn
5: Venus in Aquarius	Mercury in Taurus
6: Mercury in Aquarius	the Moon in Taurus
7: the Moon in Aquarius	Saturn in Taurus
8: Jupiter in Gemini	the Sun in Virgo
9: Mars in Gemini	Venus in Virgo
10: the Sun in Gemini	Mercury in Virgo
Page: potential of air signs	potential of earth signs
Knight: Gemini	Virgo
Queen: Aquarius	Taurus
King: Libra	Capricorn

Insight

The 56 cards in the Minor Arcana each signify how you are experiencing and expressing your energy in your daily life. The Aces and Pages are each associated with a triplicity. The pip cards are ruled by planets in signs, and the upper court cards are governed by astrological signs.

10 THINGS TO REMEMBER

1 *Tarot cards each have an astrological allocation and resonance.*

2 *The tarot was known in the fifteenth century as Tarocchi.*

3 *Tarocchi was a card game invented for the Visconti family in the court of Milan.*

4 *In the eighteenth century, occultists developed the tarot as an esoteric tool.*

5 *There are 22 Major Arcana cards and 56 Minor Arcana cards in the tarot.*

6 *The four suits of Minor Arcana cards are associated with the elements.*

7 *The court cards in the Minor Arcana correspond with astrological signs for that element.*

8 *The Major Arcana cards are each ruled by an astrological sign or planet.*

9 *The Minor Arcana cards are associated with the triplicities.*

10 *The astrological significance of each tarot card enhances the interpretation of tarot readings.*

20

Astrology and cosmic ordering

In this chapter you will learn:
- *about energy and matter*
- *about how you can draw your goals towards you*
- *about how your birth chart can help you clarify your needs.*

> **Insight**
>
> Everything in existence takes the form of energy, and science has revealed that there is a pattern, purpose and sense of order to all forms of energy. What you see and experience is governed by your perceptions in each moment, creating your reality and setting up patterns within the psyche.

At its most subtle level, everything is energy and this energy arranges itself into particular forms and patterns that we then recognize, from subatomic particles through to giraffes, through to galaxies. Since the days of our distant ancestors, who used ochre to draw their hopes for the hunt on cave walls, humankind has sought to tap into this abundant source in order to fulfil hopes and wishes. In medieval times, alchemists strove to change the nature of energy to create precious metals from base ingredients. The desire to access a snippet of the vast universal power has always been within us.

> **Insight**
>
> You have unlimited access to the boundless universal energy, but your ability to manifest your desires is helped or hindered by your self-perception. When you allow yourself to open up to a feeling of inner connection, you then create space for the gifts of the universe to come your way.

The nature of reality appears to be fluid and the structures that our lives take is shaped by our perceptions in each moment. In a sense we create our reality. If we are confident, if we have conditioned ourselves to expect life to be good, we take a positive view of life's events and are convinced that, even in times of adversity, we can achieve our goals. If we are timid or feel undeserving, often life's gifts pass us by because we do not recognize opportunities that come our way. The same experiences, when viewed through the very different frames of a negative or a positive state of mind, will have a corresponding effect on our emotions and state of well-being.

Insight

How you feel is reflected in your perceptions of yourself and everything and everyone around you. This has the effect of shaping your reality in powerful ways. If you feel negative, everything seems to go wrong. When you feel positive, all goes well and others respond favourably to you.

Although the principles have been worked with under other names in the past, more recently the term 'cosmic ordering' has described the techniques through which wish-fulfilment can be accomplished and needs met. This term was coined by Barbel Mohr, whose book *The Cosmic Ordering Service* has generated a great deal of interest in the subject of the abundant universe. The basic principles are simple: Place an order for what you wish for, trust that the cosmos will deliver and be open to the possibility that your wish will come true.

Insight

Cosmic ordering is a method of asking the universe to deliver what you desire. This involves writing a list of your wishes, and trusting that the universe will deliver your order. The act of focusing on what you want helps the manifestation process to occur.

If you are interested in testing out this principle, you can use your understanding of your birth chart as a guide. While interpreting your chart, you will have been looking carefully at all of the diverse aspects of yourself: the inner you, your outward personality, your possessions and finances, education, home and family, friendships, creativity, relationships, health, travel and career. Through coming to understand what drives you, you can decipher what is really important to you at a deep, fundamental level. Your chart can reveal what your true needs, aims and goals are, and the gifts and talents that will help you to achieve these. This knowledge helps you to become clearer about your path in life and this is the first step in manifestation. Throughout the interpretation of your birth chart, using the exercises in this book, you will have been noting down keywords and making lists. Once you are clear about the direction you wish to go in and what you want in life, you can make a list – a cosmic order – which will help to speed up your progress.

Insight

Cosmic ordering works best when you are clear about what you want. Your natal chart is useful for cosmic ordering, because your chart provides a key to the understanding of your deepest needs and desires, and enables you to find focus and direction.

10 THINGS TO REMEMBER

1 *The universe is an infinite source of energy.*

2 *We can tap into this abundant energy in order to manifest our desires.*

3 *Since ancient times, humans have searched for ways in which to access universal energy.*

4 *Our reality is shaped through our thoughts and perceptions.*

5 *Whatever we focus on draws that energy to us.*

6 *Cosmic ordering is a method for manifesting our needs and desires.*

7 *The term 'cosmic ordering' was coined by Barbel Mohr.*

8 *Cosmic ordering involves writing a list and 'placing that order' to the abundant universe.*

9 *You increase the likelihood of receiving your cosmic orders when you are clear about what you truly want.*

10 *Your birth chart can strengthen your ability to manifest because it clarifies a deeper understanding of your wants and needs.*

Glossary of terms

Angles Significant points in the birth chart. The Ascendant, Descendant, Midheaven (MC) and Nadir (IC).

Ascendant The sign and degree that marks the beginning of the first house and is calculated through the combination of time, date and place of birth. This is also called the 'rising sign'.

Aspect pattern The pattern made in the birth chart by the lines drawn between the planets in aspect.

Aspects Significant mathematical relationships between planets, asteroids and angles in the birth chart. The major aspects are the conjunction, sextile, square, trine and opposition. Also used by some astrologers are the minor aspects, which include the semi-sextile (30 degrees), semi-square (45 degrees), quintile (72 degrees), sesquiquadrate (135 degrees) and quincunx (150 degrees).

Asteroids Small planetoids in the asteroid belt – millions of chunks of rock that are thought to be the remains of a destroyed planet and which orbit between Mars and Jupiter.

Astrological signs The 12 Sun signs or constellations: Aries, Taurus, Gemini, Cancer, Leo, Virgo, Libra, Scorpio, Sagittarius, Capricorn, Aquarius, Pisces.

Astrology The art of interpreting the configurations of the constellations, planets and asteroids.

Chiron A planetoid that orbits between Saturn and Uranus. Also called 'the wounded healer' and 'the rainbow bridge'.

Conjunction An aspect that occurs when two heavenly bodies are situated close together, within 0 to 10 degrees.

Constellation An area of the sky in which stars form a visible pattern.

Degree The zodiac and birth chart are divided into 360 degrees, with 30 degrees for each astrological sign and house.

Descendant The beginning of the seventh house, directly opposite the point of the Ascendant.

Detriment The placement of a planet in the opposite sign to its ruling sign.

Ecliptic The apparent path of the Sun through the zodiac constellations. This occurs 15 to 18 degrees around the Earth and is associated with eclipses.

Elements The basic components of manifestation are divided into the realms of fire, earth, air and water. Not to be confused with the periodic table of elements in the sciences, which deals with the constituents of matter.

Exalted The position of a planet in which it holds a powerful, positive influence.

Fall The position of a planet in the opposite sign to that in which it is exalted.

Gender The astrological signs, planets and asteroids are each considered to be either masculine or feminine. This helps you to interpret their characteristics.

Glyphs The symbols that are used for the astrological signs, planets, asteroids and aspects.

Horoscope This is another name for the birth chart. The term is also used for predictions regarding the astrological signs, which are found in newspapers and magazines.

Houses The 12 inner sections of the birth chart, which govern the areas of life.

Karma The spiritual law of cause and effect.

Logarithms Mathematical tables that are used for the calculation of the birth chart.

Meridian The circle that is projected onto the celestial sphere.

Midheaven, MC The highest point in the birth chart, where the meridian intercepts the ecliptic. In several house systems this marks the beginning of the tenth house.

Moon's nodes The degree and sign in which the path of the Moon crosses the ecliptic. The North node, or Dragon's head, is found at the point where the Moon crosses the ecliptic from south to north. The South node, or Dragon's tail, is placed directly opposite.

Nadir, IC The lowest point in the birth chart, opposite the Midheaven. In several house systems this marks the beginning of the fourth house.

Natal chart Another name for the birth chart.

Opposition An aspect that occurs when two heavenly bodies are situated opposite each other, between 170 and 190 degrees apart.

Orb The degree of influence that is taken into account for each aspect.

Planets Large, round heavenly bodies that orbit the Sun in a solar system. The word stems from the Greek for 'wanderers'.

Quadrants The four quarters in the birth chart.

Quadruplicities Cardinal, fixed and mutable. Characteristics that describe how you utilize your energy. 'Cardinal' signifies creation and action, 'fixed' signifies consolidation and 'mutable' signifies adaptation.

Rising sign See Ascendant.

Ruling planet The planet or planets that govern each astrological sign and house.

Sextile An aspect that occurs when two heavenly bodies are situated between 55 and 65 degrees apart.

Solar chart A birth chart that is calculated for noon on the date of birth, when the time of birth is not known.

Square An aspect that occurs when two heavenly bodies are situated between 80 and 100 degrees apart.

Sun signs The 12 traditional zodiac signs.

Time twins People whose birth time, date and place are the same though they are biologically unrelated.

Trine An aspect that occurs when two heavenly bodies are situated between 110 and 130 degrees apart.

Triplicities The elements in the birth chart in which astrological signs are grouped: fire (Aries, Leo, Sagittarius), earth (Taurus, Virgo, Capricorn), air (Gemini, Libra, Aquarius) and water (Cancer, Scorpio, Pisces).

Zenith The Midheaven (MC). The highest point, directly overhead.

Zodiac The area in space through which the planets move. This is divided into 12 constellations or zodiac signs.

Taking it further

Useful organizations

The Astrological Association of Great Britain (AA)

The Astrological Association brings together professional and amateur astrologers from all around the world, and the website is a very useful source of information. The AA disseminates several very interesting and useful publications, and organizes seminars and conferences.

The Astrological Association
BCM 450
London
WC 1N 3XX
Tel: +44 (0)208 625 0098
www.astrologicalassociation.com

American Federation Of Astrologers (AFA)

This offers membership to professional and amateur astrologers, and offers certificated astrology courses and study programmes as well as selling books on astrology.

American Federation of Astrologers
6535 S Rural Road
Tempe AZ 85283
USA
Tel: (001) (888) 301 7630
Email: afa@msn.com
www.astrologers.com

Association For Astrological Networking (AFAN)
This is a network and information community for astrologers.

Association For Astrological Networking
8306 Wilshire Blvd.
PMB 537
Beverly Hills
CA 90211
USA
Tel: (001) (800) 578 2326
Email: **info@afan.org**
www.afan.org

Association For Psychological Astrology (APA)
This organization is dedicated to the integration of astrology and
psychology, and offers classes, workshops, correspondence courses,
books and tapes as well as a Masters Degree and Doctorate
programme in Psychological Astrology. Membership is free and
there is also a free newsletter available through online enquiry.
Email: **glenn@aaperry.com**
www.aaperry.com

Astrological Lodge of London (ALL)
This was established in 1915 by Alan Leo. There are weekly
term-time meetings in London and the ALL offers seminars and
workshops. It publishes *Astrology Quarterly*, which is dedicated to
all areas of astrology.

Astrological Lodge of London
50 Gloucester Place
London W1
Email: **secretary@astrolodge.co.uk**
www.astrolodge.co.uk

The Company of Astrologers (COA)
The COA runs courses, seminars and a correspondence course,
some of which lead to certificates and diplomas. These include
different areas of astrology and also other study programmes such
as the tarot and I Ching.

The Company of Astrologers
PO Box 792
Canterbury
UK
CT2 8WR
Telephone: +44 (0)1227 362427
Email: **admin@coa.org.uk**
www.companyofastrologers.com

Federation Of Australian Astrologers (FAA)
This non-profit-making body was formed in 1971 to promote
contact between astrologers throughout Australia. The FAA
supports the National Code of Ethics for astrologers, publishes
research and conducts examinations.

Sylvia Wilson, Secretary
Federation of Australian astrologers
PO Box 466
Woodridge
QLD
Australia 4114
Email: **sylviaw@powerup.com.au**
www.faainc.org.au

International Society For Astrological Research (ISAR)
This is an international organization of professional astrologers,
which promotes research and has a strong database.

International Society for Astrological Research
PO Box 38613
Los Angeles
CA 90038
USA
Email: **mmacycles@email.msn.com**
www.isarastrology.com

Websites for chart calculation and astrology programs

Astrodienst
This is a very useful and valuable astrology website that is the domain of eminent astrologer Liz Greene. You can have your birth chart calculated, compare it with other charts and read through a wealth of information and articles about astrology, as well as order books on the subject.
www.astro.com

Astrolabe
You can either save or print your birth chart from this website and can also pay to license the very reputable Solar Fire astrology software in order to use it professionally.
www.alabe.com/freechart

AstroMart
This multi-lingual website has a free members' section if you choose to use it regularly. It also offers program downloads for astrology software.
www.astro-software.com/cgi-bin/astro/natal

AstroWin
This website offers free astrology programs that you can download.
www.astrowin.org

Contacts

To contact the author
Lisa Tenzin-Dolma has a website at www.tenzindolma.co.uk, which provides information about her books and through which she can be contacted.

To contact Jen Govey

Jen Govey can be contacted through her website at
www.jengovey.co.uk

You can view her listing on IMDb (Internet Movie Database) at:
www.imdb.com/name/nm0332862

Index

Image credits